MW00563330

THE MEN ON THE SIXTH FLOOR

2011 Print Edition

Please enjoy this book, and if you wish, share it with a friend. Anyone in the world can Purchase the digital edition of "The Men on the Sixth Floor" for just $10. http://www.home.earthlink.net/~sixthfloor/

Copyright © 2011 by Glen Sample

Edition 4

ISBN 0-9707180-0-4

(ISBN 13) 978-0-9707180-0-6

Printed in the United States of America

Published by Sample Graphics
12901 Main Street
Garden Grove, CA 92840

Acknowledgements

In the three years it took to research and compile this book, Mark and I came into contact with many individuals who were more than helpful in assisting us with our efforts. First and foremost, our understanding and ever-patient wives must be thanked for putting up with the many inconveniences related to this project. They not only allowed us our fantasy, but they encouraged it.

Larry Howard, R.B. Cutler and Robert Johnson from the former JFKAIC were most helpful. If it were not for these gentlemen we may never have found our man and the story he bore.

John Small – mild mannered reporter – was instrumental in getting to the truth and helping us lay it out.

Thanks too to the Hunter family who put up the whole team at their home more than once. Thanks also must be given to the many researchers, writers, reporters and witnesses that we had occasion to interview and consult with. The late Harold Norman was extremely helpful as well as Stephen Pegues, William Weston, Larry Hancock, Larry Chenault, Lyle Sardie and a host of others. But without the help of Lawrence Loy Factor, who, after living for 30 years in fear, decided that the time had finally come to tell his story – and Madeleine Brown, who helped us put that story into perspective – there would be no knowledge of the men on the sixth floor.

Glen Sample and Mark Collom

CONTENTS:

Preface

If there's anyone out there who thinks the following narrative isn't being submitted to the public with a certain amount of trepidation on the part of its authors and editor, all I can say to you is "think again."

And who can blame us? After over 30 years, countless books, television specials and motion pictures, first-person accounts and revelations, and more conspiracy theories and counter-theories and twists and turns than one could shake his Ovaltine Captain Midnight Decoder Ring at, you'd think there's not much new that anyone might have to say about the assassination of John F. Kennedy.

Yes, the events of November 22, 1963 were pivotal - to some, the moment the fatal shot was fired represents the single most significant event in American history, certainly of this century - and, yes, it seems that there were plenty of groups and individuals who might have had motive enough to engineer the execution of an American President, and the nerve to pull it off in broad daylight. The problem is, it seems we've heard it all before. The names may change, the motivation may alter, but the story remains basically the same.

So why do it? Why one more book about the Kennedy Assassination? What makes us think that anyone might be interested in yet one more spin on the same old story?

As for my personal involvement, that's easy enough to answer. I was born less than six months before the death of Kennedy; I've read about his life, about the aura that seemed to surround the man during his brief time in the White House. I lived during his lifetime, yet because of a senseless act one Friday in Dallas, he is as distant a historical figure to me as Washington or Lincoln.

But beyond all that, the plain and simple truth is, this isn't the same old story. Honest. As it turns out, this is a book about the Kennedy assassination, but the focus of our attention is upon two men you've likely never heard of before now.

One of these men is the late Loy Factor, whose only real goals in life were to be a good husband and father, to make a name for himself, and in so doing, make his wife and children proud of him. The other character in this drama is a hired killer, with strong political ties, whose life ended violently in 1971. This is the story of how circumstances led these men to play a role in the most shocking crime of the 20th century, and the tragic effects their participation had later for themselves, and others around them. It is a story that has taken a team of investigators - including the authors and editor - a great deal of time and energy to piece together, and yet could never have been told at all if not for the cooperation of the man who survived in silence for three decades.

It is entirely possible, of course, that those of us who have worked so long and hard on this project have been the victims of an incredible hoax. It is possible, but I personally doubt it. Too many pieces have fallen into place along the way for any of us to discount the truth of the tale. Besides, this remarkable man stuck to his story, right up to his death, in May of 1994. There is very little reason for the subject of this story to have lied about the events in question. He had little to gain from stepping forward; and in his last years of declining health, he had little to lose as well. It seems unlikely, then, that this story is anything other than the truth this witness proclaimed it to be. I admit, however, that it is also unlikely everyone will believe this story at first. That much seems inevitable. Speaking simply from my own vantage point as editor, and on behalf of the authors and those who have participated in the investigation, all I can ask is that you read the story. Carefully. More than once, if need be. If, after you've done so, you still do not believe, so be it. We have done what we set out to do; the rest is up to you.

John A. Small

Project Editor

(An award-winning reporter and columnist, John A. Small is currently the Managing Editor of the Durant Daily Democrat, a newspaper headquartered in Durant, Oklahoma. His articles concerning the investigation into Loy Factor and his alleged ties to the Kennedy assassination earned him an award for investigative reporting from the Oklahoma Chapter of the Society of Professional Journalists in 1995.)

Foreward

"What I'm going to tell you may be hard to believe, but I am going to tell you exactly as he told me."

These were the words of Mark Collom in January, 1992, when I received his first phone call about a man named Loy Factor. The call was one of many that I received after the movie "JFK" premiered, but this call was different than most.

As Director and President of the JFK Assassination Information Center in Dallas, I have received literally thousands of calls from people of all kinds, from all over the world. Many of these calls over the past eleven years have been based on hearsay, or just plain false information. Not this one.

By the time our conversation was over, I assured Mark that I would check out his story. And check it out I did. His leads took me to Oklahoma, where the main character of this investigation once lived. Everything that I was able to find out about Loy Factor's background supported Mark's story to the smallest detail, eventually leading me to an interview with this remarkable character.

During our interview, I came to a startling conclusion: this man knows what he is talking about! His descriptions of people, places, and things related to the assassination and the scene of the assassination, ring with truth and accuracy. The questions that I asked Loy were specifically designed to weed out those who over the years have wasted much of my time. I sincerely believe that *The Men on the Sixth Floor* answers many previously unanswerable questions surrounding the murder of our beloved President, John F. Kennedy.

My gratitude goes out to Loy for having the courage to break his silence after these 30 years, and to Mark Collom for never giving up on this story.

Congratulations Loy and Mark - you are now among the few and the brave.

Larry N. Howard *(Larry Howard, who passed away in January, 1994 was the president and director of The JFK Assassination Information Center of Dallas.)*

Chapter 1
A Murder in Johnston County

Suddenly, on October 2, 1968, Lawrence Loy Factor, 43, a quiet, soft spoken Chickasaw Indian became the subject of statewide newspaper headlines. Deborah, his 15 year-old stepdaughter had led law enforcement officers to the body of her 31 year-old mother, Juanita, buried in a shallow grave, 3/4 of a mile from the family home in Fillmore, Oklahoma. She had been strangled; the belt that had been the murder weapon was found tightly wrapped around her neck. She told the sheriff's deputies that it was Loy who had murdered her mother.

Loy disappeared from sight into the surrounding woods with his 4 year-old son Donny, and for 12 days eluded an army of searchers who, with the help of bloodhounds, helicopters and loudspeakers, pleaded with him to give up. The Indian, who was not only a diabetic, but also an amputee with a wooden leg, made fools of the searchers. His skill as a woodsman and hunter served him well, as he had become the object of the largest manhunt in southern Oklahoma history. But on October 14th, Johnston County Sheriff Herman Ford and Wayne Worthen, an investigator with the District Attorney's office, found Factor and his young son. He was arrested and charged with first-degree murder.

Not able to meet the $15,000 bail, Factor was confined to the county jail at Tishomingo, until his trial - a wild media event in mid May of 1969. But an unsure jury was split in its decision 6-6, resulting in a mistrial.

A second jury found Factor guilty of first degree manslaughter and sentenced him to 44 years. He was sent to the State Prison at McAlester, Oklahoma, to begin serving his time.

Sometime in 1971, a bout with hepatitis sent Loy to the hospital ward inside McAlester. The only patient in the isolation area was Mark Collom, a young man of 21, who was likewise being treated for hepatitis. Collom was serving a short sentence for a drug-related conviction.

The young man found the Indian to be a pleasant, likable person. Mark had never actually known a murderer before but found that Loy didn't seem to fit the part. To the contrary, the man was almost simple-minded, childlike. The soft-spoken man was absorbed in an appeal to his manslaughter conviction, busily reading and asking for Mark's help and opinions on various aspects of his case. In conversations, the Indian consistently denied murdering his wife, explaining to his young friend his theory that it was his step-daughter, Deborah and her boyfriend who had committed the crime. He shared with Mark his trial transcripts which revealed Deborah's testimony to be the most damaging, while Loy often appeared to be confused and disjointed in his testimony. In the final analysis the jury believed the perjured testimony of a 15-year-old girl and interpreted Loy's mental slowness as guilt. It became clearer in Mark's mind that his new friend was an innocent man.

What was unclear however, was the motive for murder. It had been common knowledge that Mrs. Factor and her daughter did not get along, but why would young Deborah strangle her? Loy confided to Mark that he had hidden away, in an old antique corn planter, a considerable sum of money; money that he had never told anyone of, except Juanita. The family had lived on the secreted money for several years, but one day Deborah observed Juanita

JOHNSTON COUNTY
Capital-Democrat

THURSDAY, OCTOBER 10, 1968

Fillmore woman is found strangled;

Searchers fail to find suspect

Will the buzzards find Lawrence (Loy) Factor? Or is he and his four year old son alive and hiding around Fillmore? Was Factor seen entering a house in the Fillmore area Monday? In Tupelo Tuesday? In Pontotoc county? Or has Factor, alone or with the boy eluded searchers and left the area that he knows as well as he knows the back of his hand?

These and other questions remain unanswered as the steam is going out of the greatest man hunt in Johnston county history.

Organized searchers that numbered as high as 75 men were dwindling to only a few this week and Sheriff Herman Ford expressed hope some new development would permit the finding of the man who is suspected of killing his wife.

Prison photos of Loy Factor in 1977 (above) and in 1973 (right)

retrieving some of the money from its hiding place. Juanita reported this to Loy, who immediately found another hiding place for the money, but it was too late. According to Factor, Deborah told her boyfriend, Sam Davis, about the cash and the two of them began planning on stealing the money and running off together. The young, troublesome pair was a constant source of grief to the Factors. Loy speculated that the two of them tried to force Juanita to disclose the location of the money, strangling her in the process.

Juanita tried to warn her husband before her death that Deborah and Sam were up to something sinister. Loy often expressed regret that he had ignored his wife's expressions of fear and vulnerability. He also cursed the day he came into possession of that money.

The two men spent a many weeks together in the hospital. No one else was there to disturb the boredom as they talked, read trial transcripts and discussed Loy's legal strategies. As the days and weeks passed, Mark's respect for Loy grew. Eventually Mark inquired about the money. Where had it come from? Why hadn't it been used as a defense? Why was there never a reference to this money in any of the trial transcripts? The Indian was not quick to answer those questions. Mark didn't question Loy's innocence. How could a diabetic amputee, with a wooden leg, strangle his wife, drag or carry her body three quarters of a mile through the woods, and then dig a grave and bury her? Loy's explanation of the hidden money, the stepdaughter, the boyfriend, made sense - but what did not add up was why this detail was not used in his defense. It became obvious that the problem was the hidden money, and its source - something that the Indian avoided discussing.

One day, shortly before Loy was moved out of isolation, he confessed to Mark why he was unable to talk about the money, or use the money in any kind of defense.

He had withheld information even from his attorneys about the money. He assured Mark that absolutely no one except Juanita had ever known about the money, or its source. With Juanita dead, his young prison companion was about to become the only other person who knew.

Mark sat quietly and listened to Loy as he revealed the source of the money - a crime to which he had been an accomplice in 1963... a misdeed he would have avoided, had it not been for a spontaneous trip he and his wife had taken to Bonham, Texas.

(Shortly thereafter Mark Collom received a full, free and unconditional pardon from the Governor of the State of Oklahoma.)

Chapter 2
A Trip to Bonham, Texas

It was in November of 1961, Loy recalled, when Juanita read about the death of Sam Rayburn, the 79-year-old Speaker of the House of Representatives. In actuality, Rayburn had been a neighbor; hailing from Bonham, Texas, just a couple of hours away from the Factor's humble home. The funeral of the famous "Mr. Sam" was to be on Saturday and would be attended by President Kennedy. Juanita suggested they drive down to Bonham with the hope of catching a glimpse of the president and other famous dignitaries that would be arriving. Loy agreed, thinking it would be a nice trip for Juanita and the kids, so early the next morning they loaded up the kids and drove to Bonham.

Upon arriving, they determined where the best location would be to wait for the president and the other visitors, and Loy parked the family car nearby. Loy and his family positioned themselves among the hundreds of onlookers who were lining the streets, anxiously awaiting the arrival of the young president.

After awhile, the children became restless, and Juanita took them for a walk to a nearby farm implement yard, where they happily climbed around on the tractors. While she and the children were gone, a man who was also waiting in the crowd approached him and addressed him with a few words in Spanish. Loy was a dark-skinned Indian, and it was not uncommon for some to mistake him

𝕿𝖍𝖊 𝕹𝖊𝖜 𝖄𝖔𝖗𝖐 𝕿𝖎𝖒𝖊𝖘, SATURDAY, NOVEMBER 18, 1961

THOUSANDS PASS RAYBURNS BIER

Neighbors in Bonham Mourn - Funeral Rites Today

BONHAM, Tex., Nov.17 (AP) Sam Rayburn lay in state today as his friends and neighbors filed past in tribute.

These were the people from Mr. Rayburn's home town and the countryside in his Congressional district. They will attend with many of the nation's notables the funeral services tommorrow for the House Speaker, who died of cancer yesterday at the age of 79.

Mr. Rayburn's body was taken from the funeral home this morning to lie in state for twenty-four hours in the Georgian-style Sam Rayburn Library, which will be a memorial. Friends and associates, who will be the pallbearers tomorrow, served as an escort today.

By early afternoon several thousand persons had passed by the bier. They included whites and Negros.

President Kennedy is breaking into the schedule of a trip to the West to be present for the funeral in the First Baptist Church, a few blocks from the center of the town.

Vice President Johnson, a long-time friend and protege of Mr. Rayburn, will fly in from Phoenix, Ariz., where he went to attend a testimonial dinner with the President for Senator Carl Hayden.

Former President Harry S. Truman is flying down from Missouri. Associate Justice Tom C. Clark of the Supreme Court will be present.

Delegations of 23 Senators and 105 members of the House have been named.

for an Hispanic. He told the man that he was a Chickasaw Indian, and the man laughed and apologized. He was very outgoing and the two of them engaged in conversation for quite a long time. Soon after the president arrived, Loy expressed surprise at the apparent lack of security. Then the conversation turned to Factor's ability as a marksman. Loy began telling the man about his knowledge of firearms, as well as his ability as a hunter and marksman. The stranger seemed interested and pressed for more details about the Indian. He was also very friendly towards Juanita and the children, and surprised them all by slipping Loy a $20 bill and insisted that Loy take the family out to a nice restaurant. Twenty dollars was more than a day's wages for Loy. He wondered who this man was that could give away such large amounts of money.

Before the man left, he requested the Indian's address, which he jotted down on a scrap of paper. He indicated that he might have some work for Loy in the future and promised to look him up. In all, it had turned out to be quite a remarkable day for the Factors. They had seen the President of the United States, witnessed the nobility at a famous man's funeral, made a new friend, and received an unexpected gift of $20.

Over a year later, Loy explained, the stranger, true to his word, showed up at the Factor's rural home. His unannounced visit was businesslike, strictly between him and the Indian. He was more interested in Loy's ability with a rifle than making idle conversation. Loy was happy to demonstrate for his visitor, so fetching his .30-30 deer rifle the pair trudged down to a wide clearing nearby. After setting up a few bottles and an empty grease gun can, Loy gave a brief exhibition of his marksmanship. He was flawless, even when his visitor increased the target distance after every few shots. The Indian was as pleased as a schoolboy that his display of accuracy had made an impression on his guest. He enjoyed showing off his shooting skill, especially to this potential benefactor who, Loy hoped, might have employment for him.

It was then and there that the man made Loy an obscure offer that was to be the turning point in his life. The Indian's voice seemed to grow soft and regretful as he recounted the event to Mark, as if he were confessing to a priest.

The man explained that the Indian's ability with a rifle could earn him a substantial sum of money if he worked for the right people. Loy showed interest in what the man was suggesting. Nothing tangible was revealed as to the exact nature of the "work" Loy would be involved in, nonetheless the two men understood each other. Loy could shoot, and this man was willing to pay for the Indian's ability to use a rifle; offering him $10,000 - $2,000 that day and the balance paid when the "job" was finished. Those were all the details that Loy needed - and all the man was willing to offer at that point in time. He figured that the man would reveal the specifics when he was ready, for after all, there are only so many things a man can do with a rifle and get paid $10,000 for, none of which were legal. The deal was struck; the man explained to Loy that in accepting the offer, he must be ready to leave on a very short notice, anytime within the next several months, to perhaps a year.

Pure and simple greed was why Loy accepted the stranger's offer. But there was also something else - the man's confidence in Loy's shooting skills, his interest in an unsophisticated backward Indian, attracted Loy to him. Loy was now a valued commodity, needed by this man to accomplish a deed important enough to pay him big money for. After shaking the Indian's hand and assuring him that he would be in touch, the man left, leaving the Indian standing alone in his front yard with $2,000 clutched in his hand. Before the man's car had disappeared from view, Loy knew he had made a serious mistake. But he was in.

Mark interrupted his friend with a question to which he already knew the answer.

"He wanted you to kill somebody, didn't he Loy?"

"Yeah... he did. But they never told me until it was too late. I was stupid to go along with them, I got in too deep."

"Who was it Loy...who did he want you to kill?"

As the Indian responded, Mark's face showed a look of shock, and his voice caught as he tried to speak.

"I never did it though... I mean, I was there, but I never did pull the trigger."

The two men looked around their empty hospital room and then at each other. Their voices dropped to a near-whisper.

Chapter 3
A Little House in Dallas

Mark noted the Indian's facial expressions as well as his tone of voice as he continued his story. He seemed like a man who was genuinely remorseful.

Loy explained that approximately a year later a station wagon driven by a young Hispanic-looking woman drove up the muddy driveway to the Factor home. Loy described her as being around 20, very attractive, and accompanied by another young Hispanic man. She informed Loy that it was now time to put the plan into operation, her boss having sent her with instructions to bring the Indian to Dallas. It was late November 1963. He knew that he must go with them, fearing that they would kill him or perhaps his entire family if he were to back out. While he packed a duffel bag with a few belongings, Juanita urged him not to go, but Loy promised her that he would return and that there was nothing to worry about. He pretended to be calm and in control, but he was neither. The ride to Dallas was two hours of near silence. Loy was hesitant to ask anything of the pair, figuring that he would be instructed when they arrived at their destination. He pondered over what he would be expected to do - what the "job" consisted of - although it started to make no difference to him as the miles rolled by. He simply wanted to get it over with and get back home with the promised $8,000 - and his life.

It was still late morning when the trio arrived in Dallas. The woman drove to a residential area and parked. She motioned towards a small white house, surrounded by a white picket fence - explaining that this was to be the base of operations for the next couple of days. The man that Loy had met in Bonham greeted them at the door and ushered them inside. There was no doubt that this man was the group's leader.

Loy was to stay at this house for the next two days and nights. It was in this deceivingly peaceful, domestic setting that the final planning of this terrible crime was to take place, but he never fully comprehended the full scope of the plan until the last minute. Those in the group, he claimed, never trusted him and he was never included in their planning sessions.

He became more afraid than he had ever been in his life. He wondered if he had been rejected by the group, perhaps marked for murder himself. He continued to remind himself that if he were to make it out of this situation alive, with his money, he would have to keep a cool head.

Loy described to Mark how the four of them would, from time to time, be joined at the little house by two important visitors. This group, minus Loy, would gather at a kitchen table, where maps and hand drawn diagrams would be laid out and discussions would ensue into the late hours of the night.

As the Indian explained it to Mark, he was not informed of the entire plan until the last, fateful day. The young woman drove Loy to a large, seven-story warehouse building. She led Loy into the rear of the warehouse and up the north stairwell, unimpeded, to the sixth floor. There, two men were nervously checking and double-checking two rifles. One of the conspirators was positioned in the east window, while the other man - the group's leader, took up a position near the west window. Loy told of the same young Latin woman, equipped with a walkie-talkie counting down a tempo for the men, signaling for them to fire when the target reached the predetermined position. After the shots were fired, he immediately exited the building with the young woman in the same manner as they had entered. Loy insisted repeatedly to Mark that he had never pulled a trigger on that day.

Mark was struck by the Indian's sincerity. In his heart, he knew that Loy's story, as strange as it sounded, was true. There was no reason for Loy to lie about such a thing, although Mark found it difficult understanding why Loy would get so deeply involved in a murder plan without knowing, until the last minute, what the plan was all about. He also suspected that Loy was more than just a casual observer in the building, but he knew Loy to be very simple-minded and perhaps, for that same reason, very exploitable.

Further questioning of Loy ended when the two were released back into the general prison population after having recovered.

Loy Factor became one of the memories that Mark left behind, but he remained, along with his strange revelation, as someone he would not forget. And what made the story even more bizarre were the identities of the two important visitors that Loy recalled gathering with the group at the planning table in Dallas. Those men were Jack Ruby and Lee Oswald.

Chapter 4
The Loy Factor Story

When President Kennedy was struck down on that historic Friday in 1963, I was a tenth grader, making a bookshelf in wood shop class. Like millions of others, I will never forget the impact of that day - of that week - while I watched in black and white, the sad, ceremonious end of the young Presidency.

Although I came to question the official explanation of how this crime occurred, I certainly don't consider myself an "assassination buff." Never in my wildest dreams did it occur to me that I would someday be drawn into an investigation of this decades-old crime. Yet, by a series of random events, I would be. My life, crossing Mark Collom's life, was one of those random events.

I had not seen Mark in over four years. But in the winter of 1975 he and his lovely new wife, Kristi, showed up at our home in northern California. It was to be the rekindling of an old and lasting friendship that began when we were in high school together in 1965.

During our visit, Mark filled me in on the missing years of his life, his arrest and imprisonment, but most important, he described his brief friendship with Loy Factor while in McAlester Prison, a story that was to become the seed of this book. I listened with great interest as he repeated the chilling account related to him by Loy Factor back in the summer of 1971. Prior to meeting Mark, Loy had confessed his involvement to no one but his wife, Juanita. Perhaps Loy's motive in telling Mark was simply his need to purge his soul from guilt, but whatever his reason, Loy's remarkable and detailed description of the assassination and its surrounding events convinced Mark that he was telling the truth. I could tell that my friend had been totally convinced.

It was then that I recalled something I had once read in the book *Rush to Judgment*, an early criticism of the Warren Commission's Report, by author Mark Lane. Up to that point it was the only book I had ever read concerning the assassination of President Kennedy. I found the reference and showed it to Mark. In chapter 5, Lane tells of young Arnold Rowland, who minutes before the shooting saw two men on the sixth floor, and one of them was holding a rifle! "That makes sense, doesn't it!" Mark exclaimed. "It was probably Loy, or the man who hired him, that this guy saw."

I suggested that we call Dick Stewart, a friend who was an attorney and later that evening, Mark related the whole story to him. Dick was fascinated with it, and suggested that we tape record it, which we did the next day. Then we discussed our options for dealing with the information. Should we contact the FBI, the Secret Service, or the CIA? How about contacting Edward Kennedy? The decision was finally made to send the tape to a friend of Stewart's who was an investigative reporter in Los Angeles. Our reasoning was that the news media was responsible for blowing the lid off the recent Watergate scandal - not the government. Perhaps in the hands of the media, we hoped, the same results would occur.

Months went by without a word from the reporter. We finally assumed that he had run into a dead end and had dropped the investigation. We couldn't help but wonder if Loy was still alive. Had the reporter found him and determined that there was no validity to the story? We never found the answer.

The Loy Factor story was never forgotten, however. In 1992, the movie *JFK* had America talking about the Kennedy assassination again. Magazines, newspapers, and television programs dealt with the controversy in one form or another. In a *Life* magazine article on the assassination, Mark noticed a picture of Larry Howard, a consultant for the movie *JFK*, and the director of the JFK Assassination Information Center in downtown Dallas. Mark called Dallas and got in touch with Larry, explaining that he had information about the assassination that he felt could be useful. While Mark told him the story, Larry listened carefully, jotting down notes, names, and dates. He was impressed with the information and promised to investigate. Mark immediately called me from his home in the Midwest. We were both excited. Finally, after 17 years, a knowledgeable investigator was going to look into the Loy Factor story.

Within a couple of weeks Larry called Mark back. He had driven north to Tishomingo, Oklahoma and talked with Mr. John Small, the reporter/columnist with the Johnston County *Capital-Democrat*, a local weekly newspaper. John searched the paper's archives for any information about Loy, the murder of his wife and the subsequent trial. Larry also went to the county courthouse to obtain information, and although he was unable to determine whether Loy Factor was still alive, he was able to verify details of the manhunt and murder trial. Larry was determined to look into the case further.

Meanwhile, Mark and I had been trying to locate the tape made back in 1975 for Dick Stewart. We discovered that Dick had passed away and, with him, hope of ever finding the tape or the reporter he had sent it to.

Later, as events unfolded, Mark and I flew to Dallas to meet with Larry Howard at The JFK Assassination Center. We then drove to nearby Tishomingo, Oklahoma in an effort to locate Loy Factor.

The trip to Tishomingo proved most interesting. We met with John Small and the staff of the *Capital-Democrat*, and checked out several old newspaper articles concerning Factor's arrest and trial. One of the clippings highlighted the fact that Loy was a skilled woodsman and hunter. Other articles verified many of the things Mark had been told by Factor while in the hospital, such as the night that someone shot at him, wounding him in the arm, while still in Johnston County Jail. We also verified, just as Loy had said, that he was captured after the largest manhunt in southern Oklahoma history! Several other articles recounted the trial, verifying Loy's testimony that pointed to his stepdaughter Deborah as the murderer. A humorous note to the trial was the county sheriff's interruption of the proceedings to ask for the key to the jail - it was in Loy Factor's shirt pocket. Since Johnston County did not have the funds to hire a jailer, Factor, a well-behaved prisoner, was given trustee status, complete with the jailhouse key! Mark's faith in Loy's truthfulness grew. The public record was substantiating everything that he had been told, including the events that seemed far-fetched, such as Loy's possession of the jailhouse key.

Then, finally, we located Factor's sister-in-law, who pointed us to where Loy was living. We were also given his landlord's phone number, and a call that evening verified our hopes; Loy Factor was still alive! The distance was too far to drive on our short schedule, so we made plans to fly there as soon as possible. It was decided that Mark and Larry Howard would go together to talk to Loy, equipped with a tiny tape recorder. We all wondered what his reaction would be. Would he deny the story? Would he even talk to them?

It was during this period that the idea of writing *The Men on the Sixth Floor* was born. We decided that if Loy cooperated, and admitted his participation in the assassination, we would urge him to break his silence of thirty years, and come forward to tell the world what he knew. We felt the anxiety of standing at the proverbial crossroads. Time seemed to stand still while arrangements were made to contact Loy.

Chapter 5
The Factor Tapes

When Mark and Larry finally reached Loy's home on February 11, 1993, they were surprised to find that he had developed a serious heart problem and was at a nearby hospital. The two men, along with Ron Atteberry, another researcher, drove to the hospital and walked into Loy's hospital room, tape rolling. Loy was, to say the least, surprised by his visitors, but was very friendly, and after a few minutes of conversation began to remember Mark - it had, after all, been over 20 years. To assure Loy that he believed him to be innocent of his wife's murder, Mark said:

> "I don't know if you remember me, but I spent a lot of time up there with you, going over the trial transcripts, and I want you to know that I believe you. I believe that it was your step-daughter."

> "Yeah it was her." Loy responded.

> "I believe it was," Mark reiterated.

> "It was her, and she done all this, and I went through this whole thing..."

> "You told me that she did it for money."

"Yeah," Loy replied.

"Do you remember telling me that?"

"Yeah, her and that boy she was with."

"What was his name, Sam Davis?"

"Sam Davis - he died you know... he used to come up there and he'd hang around all the time, you know, tried to take her off. He caused a lot of trouble."

Then Mark carefully addressed the subject of the assassination:

"Loy, do you remember how you told me you got the money - the $10,000?"

"Yeah."

"That you were involved down there...with Kennedy?"

"Yeah."

"And how you went to Sam Rayburn's funeral, and that fella contacted you on the street? Remember telling me that?"

"Yeah..."

"You were involved with that weren't you."

"Yeah, I was kinda.. I was a little bit in it."

"We'd like to know the true story. It doesn't scare you to talk about it does it?"

"No."

Loy's reluctance to elaborate was understandable. Confined to a hospital bed, two strangers and one barely recognizable old friend barge in, asking probing questions about his sordid past. Furthermore, the Indian was sedated. Nevertheless, his memory was still sharp enough to recall many details of the past.

"What did they pay you the $10,000 to do?"

Loy stammered through an unconvincing explanation of how he merely assisted the group, that the woman was the radio operator, Oswald and the man who hired Loy were the shooters and that he had been nothing more than some sort of back up.

He reaffirmed the story of Sam Rayburn's funeral and his chance meeting with the stranger, the target practice incident, and his being picked up and driven to Dallas two days before the assassination. He told of the little house that served as the base of operation and individuals at the house, including the appearance of Jack Ruby and Lee Oswald. He stated that after the shots were fired everyone but Oswald escaped out the back door of the book building, with he and the young woman leading the way.

Larry Howard prodded Mark to ask the Indian about the elevator.

"Did you use the elevators or the stairs?" Mark asked.

"We went by stairs."

"So you went out the back of the building?"

"Yeah, back towards the north side." (The back door did face north. Loy was very exact when it came to directions.)

Larry excitedly joined in the questioning.

"What did the back look like when you went out...when you went out the back, north?" Larry inquired.

"It was kind of empty-like. It looked like some kind of dock."

"Dock?"

"Yeah... dock."

"Like a loading dock?"

"Yeah."

"Was it concrete?"

"It was like a porch, kinda like a porch."

Mark, Larry and Ron looked at each other, and then at Loy. Larry was impressed with this small detail that the man had just related. How did this Indian know that in 1963 the Texas School Book Depository Building had on its north side a loading dock? (It was later removed)

"This guy knows what he's talking about," Mark whispered to Larry.

Loy added that when he exited the back of the building, no one was there since everyone was out in front watching the motorcade. Loy and the young woman got into a car and drove away from the scene. The woman then drove Loy to the Greyhound Bus Depot.

"The bus depot is where Oswald went after the shooting," Larry informed Mark.

When Loy Factor was asked about his exit from the Depository he described a loading dock area on the north side of the building. This extremely rare photo of the rear of the School Book Depository shows a loading dock that was later removed when the building was remodeled. Loy's description of the building was amazingly accurate.

Still photo from old newsreel, courtesy of Scott Myers

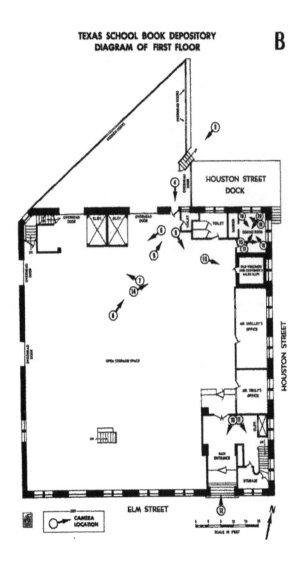

A Diagram of the TSBD first floor appeared in
the Warren Report. Notice the Dock – top right.

Loy was getting very tired at this point, and so the interviewers decided to cut it short, and come back the next day, to which Loy agreed. At this point, before leaving, Mark exhorted Loy to allow us to write a book about his involvement with the assassins, the truth about his wife's murder, and his life story. Loy consented, but insisted that if any story was written, it must contain the truth. Mark assured him that finding the truth was the very reason he had come all the way to Oklahoma.

The next morning the trio arrived at the hospital with a list of more questions, but were informed by the nursing staff that Factor no longer wished to see the visitors. Mark was disappointed, but was heartened when Larry reminded him that the Indian's reaction was quite normal under the circumstances. He had probably pondered overnight about what he had told his three visitors and had become afraid. We decided to give it a rest for a few weeks, then make a written request for another interview. Under the circumstances that was all we could do.

Weeks later, to our delight, Loy responded favorably to our request. He had been released from the hospital and was back home again. With Loy's fragile health temporarily in our favor, we made immediate plans to fly to Oklahoma!

Chapter 6
The Second Interview

Mark and I prepared to interview Loy Factor for his second time - my first. I listened repeatedly to the tapes of the first interview, and then carefully prepared a list of questions. I also began to read a mountain of assassination books and articles. The more I read, the more Loy's account of the assassination seemed plausible.

The readily available eyewitness testimony suggests more than one person was on the sixth floor of the Texas School Book Depository Building. Earlier I referred to Arnold Rowland, a young married man, who was in Dealey plaza with his wife to see the motorcade. He stated that he saw two men on the sixth floor, one with a rifle minutes before the flurry of shots struck down the president. But Rowland was not alone in this observation. Carolyn Walther, waiting for the arrival of the president at a position on Houston Street, noticed two men in an upper story window of the depository about five minutes prior to the assassination. One of them wore a brown suit coat, the other wore a white shirt and held a rifle in his hands. Like Rowland, she assumed that the men were part of the president's security detail.

Another witness, Richard R. Carr, a steel worker, reported seeing a man wearing a tan sport jacket and horn-rimmed glasses, standing in a sixth floor window, minutes before the shooting. After the shooting he saw the same man walking away from the scene on Commerce Street.

Ruby Henderson, who was across the street from the depository, recalled a similar scene as the above examples - two men.

A prisoner on the sixth floor of the Dallas jail, John Powell, stated that he, along with other inmates, observed two men on the corresponding floor of the School Book Depository Building, one of whom appeared to be Latin.

The bulk of the evidence seemed undeniable - at least two people were on the sixth floor shortly before the shots were fired at the president, and one of them is often described as dark-skinned. Loy Factor was a dark-skinned Indian and the man who hired him was also described as dark-skinned.

We hoped to find out more about the man who recruited Loy. Who was he? What was his name? Who was the young Latina? How did Jack Ruby fit into the picture? We wondered if Loy would be willing to divulge these details.

Loy greeted us from his wheelchair as we entered his humble mobile home, situated on a rural northern Oklahoma farm. A light snow was starting to fall while Mary, Loy's wife of five years, stoked up the wood stove and asked us to sit down. This was my first meeting with Loy Factor. He seemed older than his 67 or so years, probably due to the hard life he had lived, but also because of his fragile physical condition. In addition to heart disease, he suffered from diabetes. In 1964, one leg had been amputated below the knee, and recently half of his remaining foot had been removed. He spent his days in a wheel chair, relying on Mary and his sons to care for him.

He appeared comfortable with Mark, but somewhat unsure of me. Together, Mark and I assured him that his decision to relate the details of his knowledge of the assassination was the right thing to do. He needed the occasional encouragement that we would give him. He said that he had spent many hours pondering over what to do. It would have been much easier to deny any association with the assassins of President Kennedy, but he knew that it was important to come out with the truth, now, while he was still alive. His recent illness and hospitalization had made him think seriously about many things, especially the events of 1963 and the murder of his wife five years later. He apologized for having turned us away at the hospital, explaining that he had been startled by the visit, and was simply too weak and sedated to deal with any more questions at the time.

In his memory was locked away so much that needed to be told. Loy felt it was an omen that Mark and the other researchers showed up as they did in his hospital room. He had been thinking soberly about what he was about to tell us. Loy called it "studying."

He said, "I sat here the last few nights studying all that went on back then. The name of that man that I met in Bonham was Wallace, and the girl... her name was Ruth Ann."

Mark and I looked at each other. We had come to the right place.

For the rest of the day, Mark and I sat in Loy and Mary's living room, listening while Loy unfolded his story. He had so much to tell us that we had to slow him down and carefully focus our questions, as he tended to ramble. He was extremely hard of hearing. Also it was sometimes difficult to understand what he was saying, but well worth the extra effort required. We wanted to know more about this man and woman that Loy had referred to as Wallace and Ruth Ann. What did they look like? He described Wallace as a dark-skinned man, about the same coloring as himself. (Loy was a medium dark-skinned Chickasaw Indian, but looked somewhat Hispanic.)   Wallace spoke both Spanish and English and Loy assumed that he was Cuban or Mexican.   He pointed towards me and said that Wallace was about my size - six foot, 200 pounds.   He didn't know if Wallace was his first or last name, he was just called Wallace.

"How old would you say he was?" Mark inquired.

"He was older than I was...I was about 35 or 36."

"How much older?"

"He looked about 40 or 45 I would guess."

"What about Ruth Ann...the girl?

"Ruth Ann was about 20 years old Loy estimated. She was definitely Hispanic, very pretty too, the Indian recalled.   The first time he saw her was a few days before the assassination when she drove into the Factor's yard and notified Loy that Wallace had sent her to pick him up.   She was a very nervous young woman, cold and preoccupied with her mission.   With her was another Hispanic young man who Loy had never seen before.   He couldn't remember his name, but he too spoke Spanish.   They were edgy and unsure about Loy, and rarely spoke to him during their days spent together.   Ruth Ann appeared to be second-in-command to Wallace.

Loy's first meeting with the man at Sam Rayburn's funeral was also discussed in detail.   Had the meeting been just a random event? Loy seemed to think so. The man simply moved over to where the Indian was standing, waiting for the president's arrival, and attempted to start a conversation in Spanish, assuming from Loy's appearance that he was Mexican. He appeared to be alone. Would he be able to recognize the man if he ever saw him again, we asked?

"Oh god, yes!" was Loy's animated reply. "I'll never forget that man."

"Did he say anything about Kennedy in your conversation with him; did he express any hatred towards the president?"

"No, he never said anything about that, he just said Kennedy didn't have much security, and he could probably just walk up to him, real close."

"He talked about how close he thought he could get to the president?"

"Yeah, and I said he could get shot real easy by someone in the crowd."

"You told me in the hospital that you bragged to him about being able to shoot," Mark added.

"I told him I hunted and fished," Loy said.

"But did you discuss your knowledge of guns with him?" Mark asked.

"Yeah, I think that's why he told me he could use me."

"What kind of a person did you think he was?"

"Well, at first Juanita and me, we both thought he was a good man, because he gave us $20 to buy something for the kids...I thought he was rich and I told Juanita that he might have a job for me."

Loy Factor's manner of expressing himself was child-like at times, very simple, like the man himself. Sometimes he was confusing in his explanation of things. It was the same simple-minded way of his that caused a jury to eventually convict him of manslaughter at the word of his stepdaughter. His mental abilities were never fully understood back in the 1960's, when terms such as learning disabilities, attention deficit disorder, and similar handicaps were not understood. Part of a Johnston County *Capital-Democrat* newspaper article of that era helped in our understanding of Loy :

"Not much is known about Loy Factor: .... he has a metal plate in his head as a result of a shrapnel wound, according to a brother. Factor was a veteran of World War II, and in June, 1948, the Veterans Administration said he was incompetent and entitled to receive compensation in the amount of $60 per month, but a guardian must be appointed before the monies would be released. His mother, Annie Holden Factor, then filed a petition for appointment of a guardian to manage his business affairs.

Since 1950, Eddie Blanton of Milburn has acted as Factor's legal guardian. Factor's checks from the V.A. were increased to $76.75....he is a skilled woodsman, hunter, and fisherman, likes living in the woods and sometimes took his entire family out of the house to live for long periods in the woods. The family's house is a run-down affair but a new house was being constructed for Factor under an Indian housing construction program in progress at Fillmore.

Factor had his left leg removed below the knee during surgery at Johnston Memorial Hospital in June, 1964. He was bitten by a copperhead snake in 1957 while working on a ranch near Milburn, and the wound never healed.

He had many admissions into the Veterans Hospital in Oklahoma City and the Indian Hospital at Talahina for skin grafts which did not take. Factor is a diabetic, and wounds of the extremities are difficult to heal of those with the disease.

Following surgery in Tishomingo, Factor was admitted to the Veterans Hospital in Oklahoma City again where he was fitted with an artificial leg and received physical therapy until he learned to walk again." - Capital-Democrat - October 10, 1968

Sitting in his living room, listening to him speak of these old memories that he had tried to bury, we realized that his guilt must have been so heavy, that he had convinced himself that he was not really a party to the assassination of President Kennedy. He would continue to distance himself from the shooting, trying to convince us that he was merely an observer, a stand by, not really connected to the crime itself. There was a barrier that we were never able to quite break through. We were never able to extract a statement from Loy clearly explaining his specific role in the assassination. He would become very vague and withdrawn when the subject was broached. Common sense, and all of the surrounding circumstances seemed to point to the Indian as one of the gunmen on that terrible day, but Loy was never able to verbalize that. He was like a child, who refused to admit to a wrongdoing, even when the evidence was obvious.

"It was Juanita's idea to go to Rayburn's funeral", Loy said. The service was to be held on Saturday, November 18, 1961. She asked Loy how far it was from Wolfe City to Bonham, as they had often been to Wolfe City to buy seed. Together they decided to take the kids and go see President Kennedy.

Now, looking back, Loy figured that Wallace had been stalking the president on that very day, working out a plan that would come to fruition almost two years later.

Mark and I had the distinct impression that Wallace, whoever he was, recognized the Indian as an especially suitable pawn in his dark plan, for here was a man who appeared to be not only naive and simple-minded, but also a crack shot! Easily manipulated with money, the dirt-poor Indian could have just as easily been the expendable member that Oswald proved to be. In his chance meeting with Factor, Wallace must have instantly seized upon the idea that Loy was the type of person he would need someday.

According to Loy, there was no further contact by Wallace until approximately a year later, when he drove to Factor's Fillmore home. Loy walked out to meet the man and was invited into the man's car to talk business. While not remembering the details of their conversation, the substance was that his future employer wanted to see for himself the shooting abilities of which the Indian had bragged. After getting his .30-30, Loy and his visitor went to a nearby clearing to shoot at cans. Wallace was greatly impressed by Factor's marksmanship and repeating the story he had told earlier, the deal was struck between the two men. Mark then asked Loy:

"Did you know that they were going kill the President?"

"I figured they was going to shoot someone, but they never told me who it was."

"You never knew that Kennedy was their target?"

"Not until the very end."

Some might find it hard to believe that Loy would involve himself with Wallace and his group and not know who it was that was going to be killed, but this was the story that Loy Factor stuck to right up to his death in May of 1994.

Ruth Ann, Loy assured us, was one of the key people in the group.

"She knew everything about what was to happen. She helped plan everything I think," Loy said.

"She picked you up at your place?" I asked.

"Her and this other fella...I can't remember what his name was."

"What kind of car were they driving, do you remember?"

Loy thought hard, looking upward and shaking his head slightly. "I couldn't say for sure what kind it was, other than it was a station wagon, and it was a rusty red kind of color, maybe brown."

"Are you sure it was a station wagon?"

"It was a station wagon, but I don't remember if it was a Ford or a Chevy or..."

"... Rambler?"

"No, it wasn't a Rambler."

"But Ruth Ann drove, right?"

"She did all the driving. When anybody went anywhere, it was always her that drove."

"But when Ruth Ann and this other man drove up to your place to pick you up, what did they say?"

"She just introduced herself and said that Wallace had given them orders to come and get me. She said that they didn't have much time, and told me to pack some stuff and get going."

"Did she tell you to bring a gun?"

"No."

"What did Juanita say?"

"O god, she cried and told me not to go with them. She didn't want me to go, because she knew that man was up to no good."

"Why did you go?"

"I wanted the money," he said in a lowered tone.

"Were you afraid?"

"Hell yes! I thought they might kill me."

His expression about his fear of being killed reminded me of something I had read in one of the newspaper articles.

"We read that someone did try to kill you while you were in Tishomingo jail." I flipped through a folder full of research information and handed him a copy of a *Johnson County Capital-Democrat* article dated October 16, 1969:

SHOOTING OF FACTOR IN JAIL PROVES A PUZZLER - News Note: Lawrence Factor, while being held in the Johnston county jail was shot in an arm about 4 a.m. last Friday by an unknown gunman.

Who shot Lawrence Factor in the arm before dawn last Friday morning and brought a temporary delay in his trial for murder? Was it an enemy of Factor, a friend of Factor, or Factor himself?

Now that the trial is over perhaps some of the mysteries will be explained how Factor came to receive a superficial wound in the upper left arm from a spent .32 caliber bullet while he was supposed to be in a cell in the unattended county jail.

Factor told Sheriff Herman Ford and Wayne Worthen, investigator for the district attorney's office that about 4:30 a.m. Friday he was attracted to the window of his cell by an unknown young man's voice calling "Mr. Factor." A light was on in Factor's cell and he could not see who was out in the dark.

If the shot came from outside the cell it came from outside the 'walk around fence' about 15 feet from Factor's window. There were no tracks between the fence and the jail building. The bullet passed thru, without nicking a diamond shape steel mesh only 3/4 of an inch wide at its widest point, which covers the cell window. The bullet then passed thru a cardboard container of hair grease, supposedly sitting on a steel ledge connecting bars over the window, before coming to a stop in Factor's arm without even entering a muscle. The bullet was removed whole at the hospital here. It was shot from a poorly rifled gun.

Loy laughed out loud as he read the clipping.

"If it wasn't for that Royal Crown hair dressing, I might have been a dead man."

"Do you have any idea who it was that shot you?"

He explained that it may have been Debby and her boyfriend, Sam Davis, or maybe just someone who wanted to avenge Juanita's murder. It was also possible that some member of the conspiracy was sent to kill him.

"But I don't think it was them, 'cause they wouldn't have missed," the Indian noted.

The spectre of Lee Oswald being shot down, while handcuffed in the Dallas jail came to our minds as we listened to Loy. Whoever it was that tried to kill Loy that Friday morning will probably never be identified, but the similarities can hardly be ignored. It is a rarity in American society, for a man to be gunned-down while in police custody. But if that man has sensitive information capable of injuring important people, then a way will be found to silence them, whether in jail or out.

Getting back to our point of departure, Mark asked:

"So you were afraid of them killing you if you didn't go along with their plan, right?"

"That's right," Loy assured us.

"So you packed a bag?"

"A duffel bag."

"Where did you go then?"

"We took highway 48 over and then down to Dallas. We stopped in McKinney to eat."

"Did they talk to you...tell you about the plan or anything?"

"No, they mostly talked to each other in Mexican. They didn't trust me much."

"So you still didn't know the whole plan... not until you reached Dallas?"

"No. We drove to this little house I told you about. That's where all of them went over the plans."

On a Dallas city map Loy tried to show us the area where he thought the house used by the group was located. He remembered it being only several blocks away, and northwest of the Texas School Book Depository Building. Now that area is covered by commercial buildings, but there once was a residential area there, according to Dallasites we talked to. Our hope of taking Loy to Dallas and reconstructing many of his old memories was never realized, due to his weakened health condition.

"Do you remember if it was raining around the time you went to Dallas, or if the roads were muddy?" I asked.

Loy thought it might have been raining and the rural roads in his area muddy at the time. Loy's home was located in an area of Oklahoma located near the Texas/Oklahoma border. The Red River forms a natural border between the two states and the soil in this Red River Valley area is known for its unique red color. When it rains, automobiles are often covered with this bright reddish mud.

The reason I asked Factor about this was prompted by a reference I had read in the Warren Commission report regarding a couple of suspicious automobiles, covered with red mud, in the area of the assassination. Mr. Lee Bowers, a railroad employee located in a 14 foot railroad tower, spotted three cars in the railroad yard area, shortly before the assassination. Two of them were covered "up to the windows" with red mud. Another car, (with no mud on it) was driven by a man who apparently spoke into a microphone as he drove around the parking area immediately behind the grassy knoll. One of the muddy cars was remembered by Bowers as being a 1959 blue and white Oldsmobile station wagon.

"When you arrived at the house, who was there?"

"Wallace was waiting for us."

"And this was two days before the assassination...that would be November 20th? Wednesday?"

"I think it was two days."

"Did you stay at that house overnight?"

"Yeah, I slept there a couple nights. Wallace stayed there, Ruth Ann and the other fellow stayed there too."

"When did Ruby come to the house?"

"He would come by every once in a while... two or three times."

"Was Oswald with him?"

"A couple of times."

"They were together?" Mark asked.

"Yeah."

"They all discussed the plans together?"

"That's right. There was a big table at that house, and Ruth Ann, she drew out these diagrams and maps of where the cars were coming from, and which way they was gonna go."

"Oswald was in on that meeting?"

"Yeah, a couple of times, always with Ruby though."

"Do you remember the drawings and maps?"

"I didn't get to see much of what they were laying out on the table in there. They was layin' out on this table and They would gather around the plans on the table," Loy demonstrated with arm gestures.

"You said that they all spoke Spanish... did Oswald?"

"Yeah, some of the time."

"Did Ruby speak Spanish?"

"I don't think so."

"What part did Ruby play?"

"I don't know, but one day he came in, and he was real mad, and he tells Ruth Ann: 'The route's been changed, the route's been changed!'"

"He was worried that the route was changed? What day was this?"

"I think it was the day before."

"So what happened?"

"Ruth Ann says: 'I'll be back in a little while, I'm gonna go check it out.'"

"So where did she go?"

"I'm not sure, but she came back in a little while...maybe an hour and tells everyone that the route's the same...no change."

"What did Ruby say?"

"He told Ruth Ann: 'You better make sure everything goes right, otherwise we're all dead.' "

So, what Factor witnessed in this pre-assassination time period was Ruby becoming rattled by some rumor or report that the whole motorcade would skirt by the Depository - out of the range of Malcolm Wallace and the sixth floor team.

Was there reason for Ruby to become agitated?

Yes, for although one of the two Dallas daily newspapers announced the correct route to its readers, (*The Dallas Times Herald*) it's competitor, the Dallas Morning News, described the route INCORRECTLY in two of its editions!

On Friday morning of the assassination the latter published a diagram that eliminated the zig zag turn onto Elm Street altogether. It is entirely possible that one of these wrong news reports is what so startled Ruby into doubting his own "inside" information.

"Did you ever talk to Ruby?"

"No."

"How did the others view him?"

"They all respected him I think."

"But he wasn't actually part of the assassination."

"No, I don't think so...Ruth Ann, she did most of the planning I think...she knew everything."

"Was Jack Ruby with the group at the time of the shooting?"

"Not with us. I don't know where he was."

"But he obviously had some knowledge of the motorcade route."

"He and Ruth Ann both, 'cause she left the house to check on the route and then told Ruby it was OK, no change."

"Do you think Ruth Ann had more authority than Oswald or Ruby?"

"I think so. It was her mainly, but Wallace was the one in charge."

"Now, on the day of the assassination, how did you get to the depository building?"

"Ruth Ann drove, and I went with her."

"Just you and her?"

"Wallace and Lee were already up there."

"They were both already up in the building?"

"Yeah."

"Then what did you do...she parked the car, right?"

"Yeah, behind the building."

"Facing which way?"

"East, I think."

"Then what did you do?"

"I followed Ruth Ann into the building."

"How did you enter the building?"

"There was a back door."

"So you went in through the back door...did you see anybody when you went in?"

"Didn't see nobody."

"After you got into the building, where did you go next?"

"We went up some stairs."

Mark pulled out a clean piece of notebook paper and, after drawing a large square, representing the building, he asked Loy to mark where the car was parked, where the back door was, and where the stairwell was located. The Indian obliged. He drew a small rectangle at the rear of the building, an x indicating a door near the center of the north side of the building and then pointed to the upper left corner of the square, indicating it as the location of the stairwell.

"So the stairs were in the north west corner of the building?"

"Yeah."

"And you followed the girl up the stairs."

"Yeah."

"How far up the stairs did you go?"

"We went to where Wallace and Lee was."

"Were they on the sixth floor?"

"I think it was."

"What time was it when you got up there?"

"It was just a few minutes before the shooting. Ruth Ann was in a hurry. She was afraid we was gonna be late."

"Did she have a gun?"

"No."

"Did you carry a gun up there?"

"No, but when we got up there, Oswald was checking out one of the rifles. He was looking through the scope, you know and then he handed it to Wallace, said 'It's OK - it's ready to go.' "

"How many rifles did you see in the building."

"There was two."

"Was one the Carcano...the 6.5...with a scope?"

"That was one of them, but the other one didn't

have a scope."

"Do you know what kind it was?"

"I think it was a .30-06."

"What kind of action?"

"Bolt action."

"But no scope."

"That's right."

"Wallace used which one?"

"The one with no scope."

"You said Oswald was looking through the scope and then handed the rifle to Wallace, right?"

"Yeah... then he leaned it against ...kinda like a table saw; he had it all ready to go."

"What was Ruth Ann doing?"

"She was talking on a walkie-talkie."

"Was she looking out the window?"

"Yeah."

"Which window?"

"There was lots of them."

"Who was she talking to?"

"I don't know."

"Were there other shooters somewhere outside?"

"She was talkin' to someone on that walkie-talkie...I don't know who it was, probably that other fella." (Referring to the un-named Hispanic companion or Ruth Ann)

"Did you hear any of what she said, or what was said to her?"

"I didn't hear, I was too scared."

"You say Oswald had a gun, Wallace had a gun, Ruth Ann didn't have a gun, but communicated with someone on a radio..."

"That's right."

"What did you have... did you have a gun?"

"I didn't have nothin.'"

"Were you supposed to stand guard? Watch for
someone coming up the stairs, what was it that you
were told to do?"

"They wanted me to shoot, but I told them
I wouldn't do it!"

Loy was boxed into a proverbial corner and was
now forced to deal with the very pivotal detail that he had
been trying to avoid. What was he doing up on the sixth
floor of the Dallas School Book Depository Building, in
association with two assassins and a radio operator
seconds before the President of the United States was to
pass within a few yards of them? To believe Loy, we would
have to accept that he was just standing there, with no gun
and no job to do. He was simply there.

"Wallace told me that if they missed, I would be the
backup."

Loy was beginning to look tired. Mark suggested
that we take a break for lunch, and resume in another hour,
to which Loy and Mary agreed. We drove into the little
town of Tonkawa and found a small diner. Our lunch

discussion was centered about Loy's denial of any participation in the assassination. He was not about to change his position.

"What does he think, that we're idiots?" I asked Mark in a frustrated tone. "I mean, here's a marksman who has been tested by Wallace, paid money to shoot the president, accompanied the team to the ambush point and then what? Asked nicely to just stand by in case they miss? And then what was he supposed to do... run over to the closest shooter, grab his gun, and fire off a few more rounds?"

"Stinks, doesn't it?" Mark said.

"I'll tell you what I think." Mark shook his head in agreement, knowing exactly what I was about to suggest. "Bottom line - Loy was one of the shooters. That's what he was paid to do - that's what he was brought to Dallas to do!"

"Talk about someone in denial." Mark said with a smile.

"That's what he's doing though, Mark. He's either blocked that horrific act out of his mind, or he's simply trying to convince us that he was just there for backup."

"If it were me," Mark added, "I would have shot over the president, intentionally missing. Think about it - How would anyone know who missed and who hit their mark?"

"Well, at least that would have been a lot more believable!"

"Maybe that's what he did do. There were some shots that supposedly hit the grass...right?"

"True," I said, "but that's not the story Loy's giving. He wants us to believe that he was just a backup shooter without a gun."

"There's one other way to look at it," Mark offered.

"How?"

"Maybe - just maybe it happened precisely the way Loy said it did!"

"Yeah, right...Loy Factor - utility shooter!"

"Exactly!" Mark exclaimed. "Loy figured we would believe the scenario because he believed it! What if Loy was duped into being on the scene with them? Maybe he was the one who was supposed to get caught by the police with the smoking gun! What if he was the expendable one. If he had been killed by the police while trying to escape - end of manhunt, end of story!"

Again, we decided not to argue the point with Factor but for the time being, until we got more information to confirm or deny his actions, we would go along with his explanation.

We resumed our interview with Loy by reviewing the pre-lunch part of our interview. Loy again repeated the stand-by shooter scenario.

"When you went up the stairs with Ruth Ann how many minutes before the shooting was it?" I asked.

"I would say just a few, maybe five."

"Did you, or anyone in the group stack boxes?"

"No, the boxes were stacked before we got there."

"When the motorcade came towards the building, where was Oswald?"

"He was at the window, with his gun."

"Where was Wallace?"

"He was by another window."

"Do you remember which one?"

"Near the middle."

"With another rifle?

"That's right."

"Sitting, or standing?"

"He was standing back from the window. She told us not to get close to the windows so no one would spot us."

"Where were you?"

"I was over by Ruth Ann, She had this walkie-talkie like I said, and she was signaling with her arm and counting,   like, one...two...go, and waving her arm down like this."

Loy moved his arm down quickly three times, as one would do in starting a race.

"So she was signaling for the shooting to start?"

"That's right."

"Where were you and Ruth Ann standing?"

"Over by the end window."

"The west end?"

"Yeah." I looked over at Mark, who was leaning forward, literally sitting on the edge of his seat, as Loy recalled the scene on the sixth floor.

"What happened next?"

"Ruth Ann counted one...two...go, and both of them shot, almost at the same time." Then Ruth Ann and I ran down the stairs."

It would be important to note at this point that the location that Factor says that he and Ruth Ann were standing affords a commanding, panoramic view of not only the gunmen on the sixth floor but also the entire area of the so-called "grassy knoll" and stockade fenced parking area and the railroad overpass. There would be no better area to coordinate the shooters, especially if there were another shooter in the grassy knoll area. If you ever get a chance to visit the sixth floor, stand in the southwest corner window and experience the sight for yourself.

"As soon as the first shots were fired, you began running?"

"That's right, I followed Ruth Ann down the way we come, and we got into the car and drove away."

"Did you see anyone on your way down, or out the back of the building?"

"I didn't see nobody, everyone was out front."

"Were there more shots after you ran out?"

"Yeah, there was a big commotion, but I don't know how many - we was runnin' out of the building."

"Where did the other two go...Wallace and Oswald?"

"I guess they went down the stairs behind us, but I never saw them, 'cause Ruth Ann and me ran out first."

"So where do you think Wallace went?"

"I saw him about an hour or two later with Ruth Ann."

"You saw him and Ruth Ann together?"

"That's right. After Ruth Ann and I left, she drove me to the bus depot, like was planned. And I was waitin' for a bus and in a little while, the two of them comes back to the bus station to get me."

"So the plan was to drop you off at the bus station, but then they changed the plan and came back to pick you up?"

"That's right. They said they had to get me out of town, 'cause things was too hot there."

"And that was an hour or two after you were dropped off?"

"That's right."

"That was when Oswald was arrested," Mark said. "Did they say anything to you about Oswald being arrested?"

"I didn't know about that until I got home."

"So they drove you home."

"Well, we was headed up through Mead, and that car broke down, right outside of Mead... I think the clutch went out."

"What did you do then?"

"Well, I just hitched it out of there. I never saw those two again, 'cause I got a ride into Durant and then I went over to where my friend Johnny Green was workin' at this toy factory. He was makin', you know, makin' Christmas toys, and he took me home after he got off work."

"Did they pay you?"

"Ruth Ann paid me my money before I got out at the bus station."

"How much did they give you?"

"I think it was $8,000, 'cause Wallace paid me $2,000 earlier."

"So the last time you saw Wallace and Ruth Ann, they were broke down outside of Mead Oklahoma?"

"That's right, I never saw them again."

Our interview with Loy continued well into the early evening hours and Loy was becoming fatigued. We had taped over seven hours of conversation about the assassination, details about his family history, his military experiences, as well as the murder trial. Before leaving we made an agreement with Loy to correspond by mail with him, as questions were certain to come up. We were tired but it had been an extraordinary day.

Lawrence Loy Factor during one of our interviews

Chapter 7
The Factor Story Confirmed

Mark and I drove back to Tulsa that evening and played the tapes for our friends that we were staying with. Joining us was Ron Atteberry, the researcher from Tulsa who had accompanied Mark and Larry on the first interview. We also contacted Larry in Dallas to report the results of our interview. When we mentioned the name of "Wallace" to Larry, there was a marked silence on his end of the line.

"Wallace?" he asked, with a surprised tone to his voice.

"Yeah, he didn't know if it was his first or last name," I answered.

"I'm almost certain we have something on a Wallace in our files."

"On Wallace?"

"I'm sure that we have a file on someone named Wallace, but I can't remember who he was connected with. Let me do some checking and I'll call you when I find something."

We couldn't have been more excited! Could this be an important connection? Perhaps a major piece of the assassination puzzle was about to be located! We replayed and discussed the audiotapes that night until 3 a.m.

Ron brought with him a videotape of a lecture given by Robert J. Groden, dealing with his photo-analysis of an 8 mm. film of the assassination scene by an amateur photographer named Charles Bronson. The Bronson film contained footage of an epileptic seizure of a motorcade spectator, 5 minutes before the assassination. Bronson had been filming in a wide-angle configuration, and in one extreme corner of the film, the sixth floor eastern windows appear. In Groden's enhanced version of the footage, simultaneous movement can be seen in three windows.

"What this film shows, I think corroborates what Loy has been telling us. It looks as though there were several people on that floor, minutes prior to the shooting," Ron explained.

The movie footage was incredible. Hurried movement by several people was obvious. I could easily pick out at least three individuals. It seemed to be showing last minute positioning by the assassins as the motorcade began its final approach toward Dealey Plaza.

"Are there any pictures that show the entire face of the School Book Depository?" I asked Ron. "If there were three windows open on the sixth floor, then that would go along with the theory of three shooters."

"I think there is a photo that shows most of the building quite clearly, plus the Hughes film may show all of the windows," Ron replied.

"That's something we need to tie down right away," Mark added. "After all, if Oswald's window was the only window open at the time of the assassination, then that shoots down Loy's story."

It was easy to see that our work had just begun. We would now need to follow every thread of the Factor story to its end - and the threads were numerous. One of them unraveled almost unnoticed.

One night while reviewing the tapes, I caught a phrase that I hadn't remembered hearing during our interview. Rewinding the tape, I played it again. Calling Mark, I directed his attention to that section of Loy's interview and asked, "Do you remember him saying that?" I played the tape again. Loy explains that when he and Ruth Ann got up to the sixth floor, Oswald was looking through the scope of a rifle, making some last minute adjustments.

"Yeah, I remember that. What's the problem?" Mark asked.

"Didn't I read about a prisoner in the jail across the street from the School Book Depository that saw two men on the sixth floor?"

We both began searching the several books that we had brought with us. Finally, Mark found the reference.

"Here it is," he said, handing me my earmarked copy of Groden's and Livingstone's *High Treason.* "Look on page 228 - second paragraph."

"John Powell, a prisoner at the Dallas County Jail just across the street from the "assassins window," also on the sixth floor, said that he and many inmates very clearly saw two men in the "assassins window," who were adjusting the telescopic sight of the rifle one of them had. One of them appeared to be a Latin."

"That's exactly what Loy said!" I exclaimed. "And one of the men is described as Latin! Wallace might have been Latin! Loy said he looked Spanish or Cuban!"

Finding corroboration to Loy's account of the assassination became common occurrences to Mark and I at this stage of our research. Each piece of information we would gather added to our excitement, fueling our desire for yet more information, to interview more people, to make yet one more phone call. One day, soon after our trip to Oklahoma, I noticed, while reviewing the tape, that Loy mentioned there being a table saw on the sixth floor. I replayed it several times to be sure. After he describes his arrival on the sixth floor with Ruth Ann, we asked Loy:

"You said Oswald was looking through the scope and then handed the rifle to Wallace, right?"

"Yeah...then he leaned it against...kinda like a table saw; he had it all ready to go."

73

What would a table saw be doing in a book
warehouse, I wondered? I called Mark.

"It seems to me I read about there being some new
flooring being laid in the Book Depository
Building." Mark said.

"I'm going to call Larry Howard and see if he knows
anything about a table saw on the sixth floor."

That was how we met Harold Norman. Mr.
Norman was, in 1963, an employee of the Texas School
Book Depository. His job was similar to Lee Oswald's, that
of an order-filler. When I interviewed Harold in 1993 he
still worked at the Depository Building as a custodial worker
for the "Sixth Floor" historic exhibit. In 1964, Norman
testified in Washington as a Warren Commission witness to
the assassination.

Mr. Norman had watched the presidential
motorcade with two workmates, from the fifth floor,
directly under the "sniper's perch." This following
transcript is from a portion of my interview with him.

"Now, you ate your lunch on the
fifth floor, right?" I asked.

"Yeah, we got up there a little before
twelve."

"Why the fifth floor? Why not the
sixth floor, or the seventh floor?"

"Well, at first, we were going to do it on the sixth floor, but they were working, they were putting down some flooring, some 3/8" plywood, so there was quite a bit of noise, and they were painting up there too."

"Was there anyone else up there besides you three?"

"No, just the three of us."

"Did you see Oswald?"

"I saw him that morning, about ten o'clock, on the first floor. He asked Jarman (James Jarman) and I what we was talking and laughing about. We told him we were talking about the president, and the motorcade, and he just laughed and walked away."

"He laughed and walked away?"

"Yeah (laughing) like he didn't even know what was going on."

"Did you work with him?"

"Yeah, I worked with him every day. He worked there for about a month, but he pretty much kept to himself."

"How many people worked with you in the building?"

"I'd say about thirty-five or forty."

"Were most of them out in front during the passing of the president's motorcade?"

"Yeah, there were a lot of them down there."

"But you were by yourselves on the fifth floor."

"Yeah, just James, (James Jarman) Bonnie Ray, (Bonnie Ray Williams) and me."

"That was the best place to watch from, wasn't it?"

"That's why we went up there."

"Now you were telling about the construction that was going on up on the sixth floor. Why were they laying down plywood?"

"They were putting it over the hardwood flooring. You see, some of the hardwood was rotting in places; it was in really bad shape."

"I see. So it was noisy up there you said. What was it that was so noisy? Were there any kind of saws, or machinery, or anything like that?"

"Yeah, they had one of those saws, you know, one of those table saws, but there wasn't any noise going on during the motorcade, everything was quiet."

"But you remember seeing a table saw up there? Where was it located?"

"It think it might have been over in the area of the windows by the east end of the building, but I'm not sure."

"That would be the corner that Oswald shot from?"

"Yeah, I think so."

"Did you help lay down the new flooring?"

"No, we went up there sometimes to move stuff around for the floor construction guys. They didn't work for the Book Depository, but if our work got slow, we would give them a hand."

"So there was an outside contractor doing the work on the floors, right?"

"Right. There was a crew of about five or six, maybe up to eight men."

"Were they only doing work on the sixth floor?"

"At that particular time, I think they were. They were planning on doing something up on the seventh floor after they were finished with the sixth floor."

"Was the seventh floor empty?"

"Yeah, we just threw junk up there."

"What did the rear of the building look like?"

"There used to be a loading dock out there. The eighteen wheelers would pull up and we would unload them there."

"Did the loading dock extend the whole length of the building?"

"I think it did go all the way, they tore that all down a long time ago, when they remodeled the place."

"Were there steps leading up to the dock?"

"Yeah there were. I think at both ends, but for sure at the Houston Street end."

"So, to enter the building from the rear, you would have to walk up the stairs to the loading dock first?"

"Right."

"The loading dock was later removed?"

"Yes, when the building was changed to a museum."

"Would it have been possible for three strangers, in addition to Oswald, to have gotten up to the sixth floor?"

"Oh sure! All they would have to do is walk up the stairs, or use one of the freight elevators."

Harold Norman, an employee of the Book Depository Building, who himself had assisted in moving boxes for the floor construction crew, had just verified that a table saw was present on the sixth floor, the day of the assassination, just as Loy had said. How would the Indian have known of a table saw had he not personally been there? It is difficult to believe that it was a mere coincidence. What about his knowledge of the building's rear loading dock, the location of the stairs and his familiarity with the layout of the building. (the rear of the building faced north, for example.) Was all of this guesswork on Loy's part? And what about Wallace? Was this also a coincidence? Our witness was growing more credible.

The late Harold Norman poses beside the former Texas
School Book Depository. Photo taken in 1993

Chapter 8
The Discovery of "Mac" Wallace

We were anxious to hear from Larry Howard about the information he had on "Wallace". A common name, yes, but we knew that "our" Wallace must have a dark complexion, weigh 200 pounds, stand six feet tall, be capable of speaking Spanish and be a marksman with a rifle.

I was back home in California when Larry called with the information. He said that he had heard about a man named "Mac Wallace" from Madeleine Brown, a Dallas resident who claims to have been the mistress of Lyndon Johnson. She, in fact, had written a book entitled *Texas in the Morning*, a story of her life as LBJ's second love. Larry suggested that we contact her personally. He told her of our interview with Factor and his naming of Wallace as the mastermind of the Kennedy Assassination. Larry gave us her phone number and told us that she would be expecting our call.

Madeleine Duncan Brown has proved to be as lovely a lady as she is knowledgeable about the life and times of Lyndon Johnson. Her claim as being the mistress of LBJ is not a new one. For 20 years, the two carried on a relationship that eventually resulted in a son (Steven) who died in 1990 of lymphatic cancer. (The same type of cancer that claimed the life of Lyndon's mother.) Their relationship, built upon dozens of covert sexual liaisons for over two decades, gave Madeleine a unique understanding of the man; but it is her knowledge of Lyndon Johnson's political career, his business and political dealings and his enormous thirst for power, that is most compelling. Madeleine's story has been reported upon by *People, Star, Phil Donahue, PM Magazine, A Current Affair, Sally Jesse Raphael, Geraldo Rivera, Playboy,* and *Penthouse Forum.* She has been interviewed by many writers and investigators of the JFK assassination, including Richard Russell, author of *The Man Who Knew Too Much,* Jim Marrs, author of *Crossfire,* Shelly Ross – *Fall From Grace,* John Sullivan – *President's Passion,* John H. Davis- *Mafia Kingfish,* Robert Groden – *High Treason,* Harry Livingstone – *High Treason 2,* as well as Craig Zirbel, author of *The Texan Connection.* She is truly a storehouse of Texas history, as seen from the inside out. After introducing myself and thanking her for agreeing to speak with me, I got right to the point:

"Larry (Howard) has probably told you about a witness that has come forward with information in the Kennedy assassination."

"He told me that you all wanted to talk to me, and I told him that I would be happy to tell you what I know, if it would be helpful."

"Well, as you know, we've been talking to a Chickasaw Indian named Loy Factor who claims to have been involved with the Kennedy assassination."

"Yes, Larry has told me about him. You say he's an Indian?"

"Yes, a full-blooded Chickasaw."

"Interesting.."

"Well, Loy kept referring to a certain Wallace during our interview. He claims that this Wallace was the planner as well as one of the assassins in Dallas."

"Malcolm E. Wallace! I knew him personally."

"You knew him?" I replied.

"Absolutely! I am so glad to hear that somebody else has connected him to the assassination... I am really glad to hear that!"

"With this Wallace character, Loy described a young Hispanic woman who would have been about 19 or 20 years old at the time of the assassination. Her name was Ruth Ann. Does that mean anything to you?"

"Ruth Ann... that name doesn't register, maybe it might later on tonight, but I don't recall a Ruth Ann."

"But you knew this Malcolm Wallace, right?"

"Yes, you see, back in the 50's Lyndon's sister, was involved in a love triangle with Wallace, and a golf pro, down in Austin, by the name of John Kinser. Wallace shot Kinser in cold blood. He never spent one day in jail; he posted a bond; he never took the stand to defend himself when it went to trial. A fellow by the name of John Cofer, one of Lyndon's attorneys, filed a one page brief, and the judge gave him a five-year suspended sentence for a capital murder in 1952... in Texas!"

"So he must have had quite a bit of influence."

"Yes he did. He worked for Lyndon, but the kind of work he did was... well, he was a bad man."

"You mean, he killed people?"

"Yes he did. Clint Peoples (a Texas Lawman) personally told me that it was Wallace who murdered Henry Marshall. Do you all know who he was?"

"Never heard of him."

"Well, Marshall worked for the U.S.D.A. He was involved with the investigation of the land deals that Billie Sol Estes was making. Lyndon was part of it."

"I've heard of Billie Sol," I said.

"Well Malcolm Wallace murdered Marshall. Made it look like a suicide."

"A cold-blooded killer," I noted.

"That's right, and I've said all along, that the other shooter in Dealey Plaza that day when Kennedy was killed, was none other than Malcolm E. Wallace. I told Larry that the first day that I talked to him."

"Is Wallace still alive?" I asked.

"He was killed in a one-car accident in Pittsburg, Texas. I think it was in the early seventies. He supposedly ran his car into a bridge abutment."

"Loy has said that Wallace spoke Spanish. To your knowledge, could Malcolm Wallace speak Spanish?"

"Yes he could."

"What did he look like?"

"Well, he had dark hair, and I would say an olive-colored complexion."

Madeleine   Billie Sol   Larry
BROWN   Estes   Howard

Madeleine Brown & Friends.

I immediately called Mark and told him about my conversation with Madeleine and her description of the "Wallace" that she knew.

"We've got to go to Dallas as soon as we can and find out about this Malcolm Wallace," was his instant reaction.

He was right. We had possibly identified the mystery man that Loy met in Bonham. Now we had to verify it, if we possibly could.

Several conversations with Madeleine also revealed that Malcolm Wallace was a gun enthusiast, whom she had seen at the Dallas Gun Club on more than one occasion in the early sixties. He was a native Texan, and Madeleine thought that his family was politically well connected. She also told us of her friendship with Billie Sol Estes, the former Texas wheeler dealer/con man. Estes, too, was a former associate of Malcolm Wallace, and knew of his relationship with LBJ.

We arranged a trip to Dallas to research Wallace, but also to meet Madeleine and to hear more about her years with Lyndon Johnson. But before we left for Dallas, Mark received another lead from Larry Howard.

"We got a letter a few weeks ago from a man by the name of Noblitt, who lives in Washington state," Larry stated. "He's got an interesting story about a former school mate from Dallas. He thinks his friend from high school is the same man shown in the "Oswald" photograph that the CIA took at the embassy in Mexico City."

"You mean the one that the CIA said was Oswald, but turned out to be some stranger?" Mark asked.

"Yeah, that's the one. Its been published in several books on the assassination. Anyway, Noblitt sees this photograph in Hugh MacDonald's book, *Appointment in Dallas*, and says, hey... I went to school with that guy!"

"Interesting."

"What's really interesting is who Noblitt's schoolmate's best friend was." Larry added.

"Who?"

"Malcolm Wallace."

Within an hour, Mark succeeded in contacting Mr. Gene Noblitt on the telephone. What Larry had reported to Mark had not been an exaggeration.

Chapter 9
The Strange Story of Gene Noblitt

You may wonder, after reading this chapter, where the story of Gene Noblitt fits into the scenario of the Kennedy Assassination. We wonder too. But to leave out this interesting piece of the puzzle would not be fair, since it is information that we uncovered along the way of our investigation. In a way, it creates more questions than it answers, but we hope that like us, you will find it just as fascinating, if not provocative.

Thank goodness for assassination books. For even though many are full of the most bizarre and often untenable theories, there are truths to be found in each one of them. Like mother used to say, "Even a broken clock is right twice a day." And so it was with the book that Gene Noblitt found one day. Hugh MacDonald's *Appointment in Dallas* presented an interesting view of the assassination of President Kennedy, but when Noblitt arrived at pages 53-59, his interest turned to shock. On those pages were photographs of a man that he knew. Locating his 1938 Woodrow Wilson High School Crusader Yearbook, Gene looked up the man's pictures. Sure enough, there was a strong resemblance to a high school friend by the name of Ralph Geb, even though there was a period of 25 years between photographs. In a letter we received, Noblitt elaborated:

"I recognized the pictures as soon as I saw them. They looked just like Ralph Geb. Actually they looked a lot like Ralph's father looked in 1938. Ralph attended Woodrow Wilson High School. He was fair skinned, light hair. Played guard on our football team. Long-waisted, short legs, he stayed in good shape. He grew up just west of the Santa Fe tracks - tough neighborhood. His father worked as a smith at Weaver Spring & Axle Company, in Dallas. When I found the picture of our football team and saw Ralph Geb standing next to Malcolm Wallace, then BONG - BONG the bells went off! I knew about the murder that Malcolm had committed in 1951, and had also heard that LBJ provided his best attorney to defend him."

Then we asked him to describe the Wallace that he knew and grew up with in Dallas.

"Malcolm Wallace attended Woodrow Wilson High School, graduating Magna Cum Laude. He was dark-complected, had dark hair, brown eyes. If he were in Mexico, he could pass as a Mexican; if he were in Cuba, he could pass as a Cuban. He was Quarterback on the school football team. He was in great shape, tough as nails. His uncle was Secretary of Agriculture in FDR's time in Washington D.C. {not confirmed) I don't know if he spoke Spanish, but he spent a lot of time in west Texas where one is used to both Spanish and English. I lost track of Malcolm and Ralph Geb in 1938 when we graduated. Malcolm went on to the University of Texas at Austin with a lot of our WWHS football players, and then into the Marines, I think. I never did hear about Ralph Geb again. I only recently heard of the JFK Assassination Information Center, and so I got in contact with them and gave them this information. You have my permission to use this material if it will help in finding the person, or persons who engineered this assassination of JFK."

We also learned that Mr. Noblitt, a Dallas businessman in 1963, had actually been around the corner from Dealey Plaza on November 22. In another note he relates:

"Dear Mark,

As per your request, this is the way I saw and heard the shooting. We, John, Jack Worley and I had been to the F.H.A. office to pick up a block of housing commitments. John Worley treated us to lunch. The sidewalks were full of people waiting to see JFK. We made the exit from the sandwich shop just in time to see the president's car streaking down Main Street. All of the people moved from the sidewalk into the street. We just moved to the curb to see the president. It was a shock to see the red-haired president riding in an open car. After all the problems in elevators, signs and newspaper notices. The other cars followed but all eyes were on the president. He looked great. The cars made a right turn. We walked across Main street. The next thing we heard was the shots. It sounded like we were in the hill country deer hunting. The deer was running and three or four hunters were shooting I made the remark "They got him." We ran to the car, turned the radio on. We heard "....the police are running up the grassy slope...the president has been shot." The rest is history. We cried all the way to the office, closed the office and went home in shock."

Ralph Geb in 1938 high school photo.
Was he the man photographed at the
Soviet & Cuban Embassies in Mexico?

This is the man that the CIA covertly photographed over 20 times entering and leaving the Soviet and Cuban Embassies in Mexico City. For some reason, they thought the man was Lee Harvey Oswald. Gene Noblitt recognized him as his old high-school friend – Ralph Geb. Geb was a close friend of Malcolm E. Wallace.

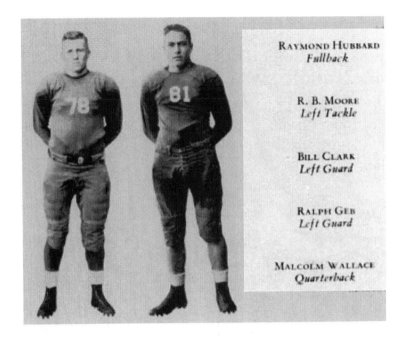

RAYMOND HUBBARD
Fullback

R. B. MOORE
Left Tackle

BILL CLARK
Left Guard

RALPH GEB
Left Guard

MALCOLM WALLACE
Quarterback

Ralph Geb with his best friend Malcolm Wallace. Photo taken in 1938 – their senior year at Woodrow Wilson High School, Dallas, Texas.

Author Glen Sample, Madeleine Brown and
Gene Noblitt, during a visit to Dallas.

Having personally met and talked to Mr. Noblitt
extensively, as well as corresponding with him several times,
I found him both reasonable as well as honest. He certainly
had nothing to gain by fabricating this information. He is as
sincere as a man can be about his identification of Ralph
Geb as the man the CIA mistakenly identified as Lee
Harvey Oswald. Additionally, he did attend the same high
school at the same time as Malcolm Wallace and Ralph Geb.

If it were simply a story about a friend who looks
similar to a man in a CIA photograph thought to be

Oswald, then I might have my doubts. Maybe a case of mistaken identity. Maybe an overly excited JFK buff, no big deal. But add to this picture the fact that Ralph Geb was Malcolm Wallace's best friend - supported by the testimony of a fellow classmate who knew them well - and you have more than a simple coincidence. In support of this is a yearbook photo showing Wallace and Geb - best friends as well as team-mates - standing next to one another. What you have are two separate individuals, who are both independently connected to the Kennedy assassination case by two separate threads of evidence.

1.) Geb is suspected of complicity in the assassination by his identification as the man in the CIA photograph, thought to be Lee Harvey Oswald.

2.) Malcolm Wallace is suspected of complicity in the assassination by testimony from Madeleine Brown.

If the CIA's "Oswald photograph" truly was that of Ralph Geb, then it is anyone's guess as to what he was doing in Mexico City on exactly the same day that Oswald was purportedly there. We have no theories to advance on this peripheral matter. Other assassination researchers have suggested that Oswald never visited the embassies in Mexico City at all, but that an "imitation Oswald" made the visits in his place, using his name. They theorize that this "Oswald stand-in" (Geb, perhaps) was therefore covertly photographed by the surveillance cameras of the CIA, posted near the entrances to the Soviet and Cuban Embassies, and that they then forwarded this information to the FBI on the evening of the assassination, only to find out that their "photographed" Oswald was not the "real" Oswald. In Dick Russell's book, *The Man Who Knew Too Much,* (1992- Carroll & Graf) this subject is dealt with. On page 496, under the subheading: THE UNIDENTIFIED MAN - we quote:

Another CIA memorandum makes reference to twenty photographs of Oswald taken in Mexico City. But only twelve pictures have ever been released - and they are all of the wrong man.

Another CIA memo, dated November 22, 1963: "Reference is made to our conversation of 22 November in which I requested permission to give the [FBI] Legal Attaché copies of photographs of a certain person who is known to you." A special flight with these photos was then made from Mexico City to Dallas via a naval attache, and more to CIA headquarters by pouch that night....

If not Oswald, then who was "a certain person who is known to you"? It came out in 1975 that the mystery man was photographed outside the Soviet Embassy on October 1, the same day that Oswald was known to have made another visit there. On October 10 the CIA had sent a cable to the FBI, the State Department, and the Navy headed "Lee Henry [sic] Oswald." It read: "On 1 October 1963 a reliable and sensitive source in Mexico reported that an American male, who identified himself as Lee OSWALD contacted the Soviet Embassy in Mexico City inquiring whether the embassy had received any news concerning a telegram which had been sent to Washington. The American was described as approximately 35 years old, with an athletic build, about six feet tall, with a receding hairline." That fit the description of the man in the picture, but it was obviously not the slender, twenty-three-year-old Oswald. But whoever it was, he appeared to have been impersonating Oswald at the Soviet Embassy gate.

Similar treatment is given by Jim Marrs in: *Crossfire – The Plot That Killed Kennedy* (1989 - Carroll & Graf, New York) We quote from page 195:

While the CIA stated that both the Cuban and Soviet Embassies were under photographic surveillance during Oswald's visits, they could offer no proof. Lamely, CIA officials explained to the Warren Commission that the camera at the Soviet Embassy was turned off on Saturdays (the day Oswald supposedly was there) and that the camera at the Cuban Embassy just happened to break down the day Oswald was there. However, the day of the assassination, CIA officials sent photos taken outside the Soviet Embassy in Mexico City to the FBI, claiming they were of Oswald. They are obviously of someone else. This someone appears to be about thirty-five years old, six feet tall, with an athletic build....

CIA officials admitted there had been a "mix-up" on the photos. The House Select Committee on Assassinations noted that Oswald allegedly made at least five trips to the two embassies and found it hard to believe that he was not photographed even once. The committee expressed the belief that "photographs of Oswald might have been taken and subsequently lost or destroyed."

The absence of any photos of Oswald at the embassies raises suspicion that an impostor was posing as Oswald during these embassy visits. (End of quotes)

Why do many feel that Oswald was impersonated at these embassies? Some speculate that Oswald, was being "painted", or set up to look like a textbook assassin. Or, that by associating Oswald with the Cuban and Soviet Embassy, the blame for the planned assassination would automatically shift to Cuba, causing a swift retaliation to that bastion of communism. Oswald certainly appears to have had a deep interest in Cuba and Cuban affairs.

How much of this was genuine and how much has been staged will remain a center of hot debate for decades, but in November of 1999 a news story broke nationwide that led many more people to believe that Oswald may have been impersonated in Mexico City. Part of the news story was that FBI director Hoover briefed President Johnson shortly after the assassination about not only photos, but TAPE RECORDINGS that had been examined by federal agents.

"We have up here the tape and the photograph of the man who was at the Soviet embassy using Oswald's name," Hoover told Johnson, *according to a transcript of that call released in 1993. "That picture and the tape do not correspond to this man's voice, nor to his appearance. In other words, it appears that there is a second person who was at the Soviet embassy down there."*

So the theory that Oswald was being impersonated in Mexico City was not originated by assassination writers, but by the FBI itself!

After months of searching for Ralph Geb, we eventually found his daughter, living in San Diego, California. She informed me that her father died in 1990, after a long career in the Air Force. Ralph's brother, Fred, was an Army intelligence/C.I.A. officer who died a few years before Ralph. "My family used to joke about having a spy in the family," she said, "but Uncle Fred would never talk about it."

Somewhere in all of this there must be a connection, but, as in many old mysteries, the trail appears cold, and growing steadily colder.

(Eugene Noblitt passed away on July 4, 1998.)

Chapter 10
The Windows on the Sixth Floor

"At the third shot he looked up and saw a 'movement' in the far east corner of the sixth floor of the Depository, <u>the only open window on that floor</u>."
The Warren Commission Report, (regarding James N. Crawford)

There are several things about Loy's account of the assassination that vary from the run-of-the-mill conspiracy theories, but the primary difference is his contention that there were multiple shooters on the sixth floor. We believe, in spite of Loy's denials, that he could have been one of the shooters on the sixth floor, making a total of three. But even if he is correct and there were only two, there must have been at least two windows open on the sixth floor to make his story valid. Three open windows would tend to support our suspicions of three riflemen. We were eventually able to determine without doubt, the **exact** configuration of the windows at the time of the shooting, thanks to a photographer who was riding in the motorcade. In Robert J. Groden's book - *The Killing Of a President* (1993 Penguin Books, New York) there are several versions of Tom Dillard's famous photograph on page 158 and again on pages 208 and 209. The photograph is in full color and shows the face of the Texas School Book Depository Building. Groden explains it this way:

"THE FIGURE IN THE WEST WINDOW - Dallas Morning News photographer Tom Dillard took a photo of the Depository that caught the building's sixth floor

windows.   Dillard, riding in a motorcade press car (eight cars behind the President's), snapped the picture 15 seconds after the last gunshot was fired. "

In addition to Dillard's photograph there were two home movies that show glimpses of various sections of the School Book Depository at that critical moment. One is the home movie taken by Mr. Bronson, mentioned earlier, the other film is commonly called the "Hughes film". Robert Hughes was standing on the corner of Main and Houston, filming the presidential motorcade as it rounded the corner and proceeded up Main Street. As the procession made the deadly turn onto Elm Street, Hughes caught a brief view of the eastern corner of the building, including the sixth floor corner windows.   Only the eastern end of the building, showing the open "Oswald" window was visible. The film then stops and then starts again, showing crowds of people running towards the grassy knoll area, in the wake of erupting gunfire. Hughes captures in a dramatic way the confusion in Dealey Plaza that day.   He then captures another look at the *west end* of the sixth floor which shows other windows open.

In our drawing and photos which follow, we show the *exact positions* of the sixth floor windows. The reader will notice that there are seven sets of windows across the front of the Depository's sixth floor. Of those seven, three are open sufficiently for an assassin to shoot out of.   One window, in the second set from the left, is slightly open, just a few inches. There were no open windows on the seventh floor.

The west corner of the TSBD showing open windows. This photo is from the Hughes film.

This photo was also shot immediately after the shots were fired. Notice sixth floor window configuration.

THE TEXAS SCHOOL BOOK DEPOSITORY BUILDING

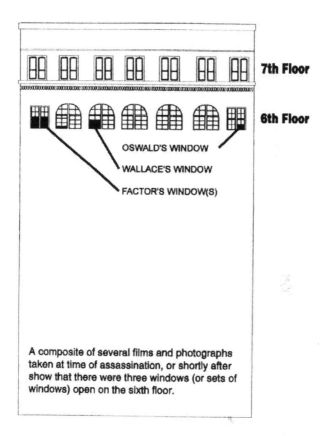

7th Floor

6th Floor

OSWALD'S WINDOW

WALLACE'S WINDOW

FACTOR'S WINDOW(S)

A composite of several films and photographs taken at time of assassination, or shortly after show that there were three windows (or sets of windows) open on the sixth floor.

FBI agents demonstrate the size and configuration of the sixth floor windows. Agent is sitting on a box of books, in the same manner as Oswald allegedly did while firing into the presidential motorcade. Note that the bottom of the window is 12 to 13 inches from floor level. Because of this window ledge height, a shooter that was positioned close to the window would have to kneel, or sit. (as shown in photo) But a standing rifleman could shoot from a position several feet back from the windows, thus avoiding exposure to onlookers below.

No witnesses reported seeing any rifle barrels from any window other than the eastern corner window. And with good reason. A visitor to the sixth floor of the former depository (also referred to as the "old Sexton Building" by old-time Dallasites) will notice the unusual layout of the windows. The bottoms of the windows are a mere 13" from the floor. Standing a few feet away from any of the Elm Street windows, facing south, one can see how a shooter, standing upright, could draw a bead on the passing president and fire his rifle without extending the rifle out of the window. He may choose to rest his rifle on a stack of books, (there were plenty of them that could have been used) or shoot without any support at all. A sniper, firing in this manner, would be concealed from the crowd below, as well as concealing any 'muzzle flash' that could attract attention.

A former military sniper I have corresponded with observed that a professional sniper, shooting from a building, would position himself back inside a room in the shadows. He would not stick a rifle barrel out of a window, nor show himself to outsiders who may glance in. The window would be open only a crack. Recall that Ruth Ann, according to Factor, told everyone to stand back, away from the windows. Oswald, shooting from a sitting position, his rifle resting on a box of books and jutting out the window, like a beacon, for everyone to see, shows poor planning, and indicates that he was probably a poor shot and certainly *not* a professional.

Recall that months before the assassination, Oswald, reportedly shot at General Walker and missed - even though his target was only a few feet away and stationary!

The photograph taken of the face of the depository by Tom Dillard was later enhanced and examined by experts. Groden reports: (page 208 – *The Death of a President)*

"This photo, widely published since the assassination, has always been reproduced with the left side (which shows the west-end windows) cropped off. The uncropped version is shown here and includes the sixth floor west -end windows. In one of them is the figure of a heavyset man wearing a white T-shirt. A shot fired from this window would match either of Governor Connally's wounds, explaining how the Governor was hit on such a sharp right-to-left trajectory at a steep, downward angle."

If Dillard's photograph does indeed show the figure of a man in the southwestern window, it should come as no surprise. It simply reinforces the testimony of other witnesses, including that of Lawrence Loy Factor.

Chapter 11
The Dallas Revelation

Our next trip's itinerary would be quite focused and straightforward. We would spend September 2 - 5, 1993, in Dallas, searching for any information that could be found relating to Malcolm Wallace. We also made arrangements to meet with Madeleine Brown for a recorded interview.

I flew into Dallas from Los Angeles, Mark from St. Louis. Upon meeting and renting a car, we went to the JFKAIC to meet with Larry Howard and to bring him up to date with the information we had developed on Wallace. He suggested the Dallas Public Library as an excellent place to find what we were looking for. As it turned out, the library was a short distance from our hotel.

Early the next morning we made our way to the seventh floor of the library where archives of *The Dallas Morning News* as well as other reference materials are located. It didn't take us long to realize we had hit pay dirt. Our goal was to find two key things: photographs of Malcolm Wallace and information relating to his life, education and background. For nearly two days, we uncovered all of that and more.

First and foremost we retrieved a front page article from *The Dallas Morning News*, dated Friday March 23, 1984. It was concerning the murder of Henry Marshall, which Madeleine had earlier briefed us on. The headline read: "BILLIE SOL LINKS LBJ TO MURDER." There were four photographs; Billie Sol Estes, LBJ, Henry Marshall and Malcolm Wallace.

Malcolm Everett Wallace. University of Texas (about 1945)

Malcolm "Mac" Wallace. University of Texas (about 1945)

We studied the photograph of Wallace carefully, as this was the first view of our subject. He looked handsome, perhaps even studious; dressed in a suit and tie, with wire rimmed glasses. Now we had something that we could show Loy! A photograph of Wallace! We read on:

By David Hanners - Staff writer of The News. Franklin, "Texas - Convicted swindler Billie Sol Estes told a grand jury that Lyndon B. Johnson was one of four men who planned the 1961 murder of an agriculture official, three sources close to the grand jury said Thursday. The sources said Estes testified that the group feared the official would link Estes' illegal activities to Johnson.

Estes, who was given immunity from prosecution to testify before a Robertson County grand jury Tuesday, told grand jurors that Johnson felt pressure to silence Henry Harvey Marshall of Bryan, a regional U.S.... Department of Agriculture official in charge of the federal cotton allotment program, sources said.

Lady Bird Johnson, the president's widow, could not be reached for comment on Estes' testimony Thursday. "All we will say is that Mrs. Johnson does not answer scurrilous attacks and comments such as that," said Liz Carpenter, who served as Mrs. Johnson's press secretary when LBJ was president.

The sources, who asked to remain anonymous because grand jury testimony is secret under state law, said Estes testified that he had attended at least three meetings with Johnson - two in Washington and one at the Driskill Hotel in Austin - during which they discussed the need to stop Marshall from disclosing Estes' fraudulent business dealings and his ties with Johnson.

Estes testified that he later balked at the idea of killing Marshall, according to sources. Marshall had resisted attempts to transfer him from Bryan to Agriculture Department headquarters in Washington in order to silence him. Sources said Estes' testimony implicated:

110

Johnson, who had just been elected vice president. Estes and his family have repeatedly said that Estes was a political ally of LBJ, and that Estes made repeated campaign contributions to LBJ's campaigns. Johnson assumed the presidency on the death of John F. Kennedy, on Nov. 22, 1963. He was elected in 1964 to a full term, but chose in 1968 not to seek re-election. He died at his ranch in Stonewall, Texas, on Jan. 22, 1973.

Clifton C. Carter, a close Johnson political aide and troubleshooter who later served as Executive Director and Treasurer of the Democratic National Committee. Carter died of natural causes in Arlington (Va.) Hospital Sept. 21, 1971.

Malcolm Everett (Mac) Wallace, the president of the 1945 student body at the University of Texas at Austin and a onetime U. S. Agriculture Department economist. Wallace, whom sources said Estes identified as Marshall's killer, previously had avoided a prison term on a 1952 murder conviction in Austin. Wallace died, sources said, in a Northeast Texas automobile accident in 1971.

A relative found Marshall's body June 3, 1961, on his Robertson County ranch. He had been shot five times, and his bolt-action .22 caliber rifle was found nearby. His death originally was ruled a suicide by a local justice of the peace, but the ruling came into question a year later when news broke of Marshall's investigation of Estes' cotton allotments.

U.S. Marshall Clint Peoples, who as a Texas Ranger captain began investigating the Murder in 1962, said Thursday that Marshall "was blowing the whistle" on Estes' scheme to defraud the government's cotton allotment program.

Peoples, who persuaded Estes to testify before the grand jury Tuesday, refused to name the people whom Estes implicated in the conspiracy.

"I asked him (Estes) why he didn't testify at the first grand jury in 1962, and he said if he had, he would have been a dead man," said John Paschall, the district attorney.

Paschall said records from the 1962 grand jury revealed that Marshall approved 138 cotton allotments for Estes from Jan. 17 to June 3, 1961. But, Peoples said, "The facts are that Henry Marshall was told to approve them (Estes' cotton allotments)." Before 1961, Estes, a Pecos millionaire who had made much of his money through federally subsidized farm programs, had become a key Democratic power broker and fund-raiser for the campaigns of Johnson, Yarborough and then-Gov. John Connally. Less than a year later, Estes' multi-million dollar empire - built on non-existent grain storage elevators and cotton allotments he obtained fraudulently - collapsed.

In March 1962, Estes was indicted on fraud charges. Two months later, U.S. Agriculture Secretary Orville Freeman said Marshall had been the only man who could provide some of the answers to questions about Estes' involvement in the cotton allotment program.

Days later, a state district judge in Bryan authorized the exhumation of Marshall's body. An autopsy by Harris County Medical Examiner Joseph Jachimczyk revealed that Marshall suffered not only five gunshot wounds to his lower left abdomen but also carbon monoxide poisoning and a head injury. The bruise to Marshall's head occurred before his death, Jachimczyk said, and would have been incapacitating."

Sybil Marshall, the wife of the slain Agriculture Department official, said Thursday, "I'm kind of shocked. I don't know what to think."

Mrs. Marshall said her family always believed her husband had been murdered. "I can't believe he would do that to himself (commit suicide), she said. "He was a good man."

Estes, despite two federal trials and subsequent prison terms in the following two decades, steadfastly had refused to discuss his relationship with Lyndon Johnson or the Marshall murder. Called to testify before a 1962 grand jury investigating Marshall's death, Estes repeatedly

112

invoked his constitutional right against self-incrimination, according to press reports at the time.

"Daddy's silence... allowed Lyndon Johnson to become president," Estes' daughter, Pam Estes, wrote in a book about her father titled BILLIE SOL, which was released last week.

"During that time, Daddy had been supplying Lyndon Johnson with large infusions of cash, not only for his own political needs but for people Johnson himself chose to help.

"Sometimes Johnson would send people like Ralph Yarborough directly to Daddy for fund-raising help. On other occasions, Johnson would get bundles of cash from Daddy and distribute it himself. Since those transactions were all cash, there is no reliable way of knowing how much money went to Johnson or what became of it.

"Daddy has steadfastly refused to talk about that part of his life with anyone, even me," she wrote. Wallace, whom sources said Estes named as the triggerman in Marshall's murder, at one time had dated Johnson's sister, Josefa, according to a friend of the Johnson family who asked not to be identified. Johnson's sister died in 1961.

However, Horace Busby, a close friend of Johnson's, said Johnson met Wallace only once, when Carter brought Wallace to Johnson's home in Washington. Wallace was convicted in 1952 of killing John Douglas Kinser of Austin. Testimony in that case revealed that Kinser had been having an affair with Wallace's wife. Wallace was sentenced to a five-year prison term, which was suspended.

Wallace was represented in his 1952 trial by Austin criminal defense lawyer John Cofer, now deceased. Cofer, a longtime LBJ confidant, had represented Johnson in the Jim Wells County "Box 13" voter fraud case in 1948. Because of the slim edge of 87 votes he received from Box 13, Johnson won a runoff election against Coke Stevenson for the U.S. Senate.

LYNDON B. JOHNSON
SENATE DEMOCRATIC LEADER

January 12, 1961

Dear Billie Sol:

The roses were lovely and they added just the touch we needed to the house during the holiday season.

Thanks for remembering us -- it's wonderful to have friends like you.

Best wishes.

Sincerely,

Lyndon B. Johnson

Mr. Billie Sol Estes
Box 1052
Pecos, Texas

THE VICE PRESIDENT

WASHINGTON

August 16, 1961

Dear Friend:

      Summertime means a lots of things -- not the least of which is ripe, delicious Pecos cantaloupe.

      Many, many thanks for your thoughtfulness.

      I am grateful.

      Sincerely,

      Lyndon B. Johnson

Mr. Billy Sol Estes
Pecos, Texas

These are two of many letters that LBJ wrote to Billie Sol Estes over the years. LBJ and Others attempted to distance themselves from the notorious wheeler dealer, but notes such as this negated their claims.

Cofer defended Estes in his 1962 fraud trial. Ms. Estes said in her book that Cofer was hired "at the insistence of Lyndon Johnson."

Cofer rested Estes' case without calling any defense witnesses. "I feel that that was done to make sure there was no opportunity of implicating Lyndon Johnson during any testimony or cross examination," Ms. Estes wrote.

"It should be clear by now that it was Lyndon Johnson who paved the way for the preferential treatment Daddy received from the Agriculture Department," she wrote.

Estes, who was in Dallas Thursday to autograph copies of his daughter's book, refused to comment on his appearance before the grand jury Tuesday. Peoples said Thursday that Estes finally had agreed to testify after Peoples arranged for Estes' immunity from prosecution. The Marshall said Estes wanted to clear his conscience about Marshall's death, and "he should be commended for it."

Peoples, who escorted Estes to LaTuna Federal Correctional Institute in El Paso in 1979 after Estes' second fraud conviction, said he had told Estes: "Billie Sol, you ought to straighten this thing out. I'm not saying you did it, but I'm saying you know who did."

Peoples said Estes told him then, "You're looking in the wrong direction. You ought to be looking at the people with the most to lose."

Peoples said Estes drove to Waco, where Peoples lives, Monday night and met with him to discuss his testimony and immunity. "This is the first time that Billie Sol has ever testified... against anybody," Peoples said.

Although he repeatedly declined to discuss the grand jury investigation, Peoples said Estes had "brought out evidence that I had in my files that he couldn't have known - except one way."

The Agriculture Department, in an attempt to reduce the surplus of cotton in the early 1960's, strictly controlled the acreage to be planted in the crop, embargoing cotton production on new land.

Estes devised a scheme under which cotton allotments, or federal permits to grow the crop, were transferred from other farmers to his Pecos farm. "Meanwhile, the Agriculture Department was in a dither," Ms. Estes wrote in her book. "They didn't know whether Daddy was legally leasing the land with cotton allotments attached or illegally purchasing allotments."

In the summer of 1961, they decided to conduct an investigation to try to satisfy themselves as to its legality....By the fall of 1961, Daddy had gotten wind of the investigation. His first reaction was to go to Washington to knock some heads together. This is something Daddy knew how to do very well," she wrote.

"This is starting to fill in," I commented to Mark. "Not bad for the first hour," he said, smiling.

Madeleine had informed us that the Wallace she knew was a killer who was covertly working for Lyndon Johnson. Now, another witness, albeit a known con man, testifies under oath to a grand jury that Malcolm was the killer of Henry Marshall at the behest of LBJ.

The obvious picture to develop from this information was that Wallace not only extricated Vice President Johnson from political ruin but also expedited his promotion to the presidency by planning and carrying out the assassination of President Kennedy.

But while Wallace was loyally ministering to the needs of Johnson, Billie Sol Estes was busily ingratiating himself to Johnson by funneling millions of dollars to an LBJ slush fund, according to another report.

Dallas Morning News - Saturday March, 24, 1984. By David Hanners and George Kuempel -Franklin, Texas -

Convicted swindler Billie Sol Estes told a grand jury that illegal cotton allotments and other business deals he arranged with Lyndon B. Johnson's help in the early 1960's generated $21 million a year, with part of the money going to a slush fund controlled by LBJ, sources close to the grand jury said Friday.

Estes, protected from prosecution by a grant of immunity, testified for 4 1/2 hours Tuesday before the Robertson County grand jury. The sources said Estes testified that in January 1961 - the same month LBJ became vice president - Estes and two other men met with Johnson at LBJ's Washington home to discuss Henry Harvey Marshall of Bryan, an Agriculture Department official who was questioning the legality of Estes' cotton allotments. ....Estes quoted LBJ as saying, "Get rid of him," referring to Marshall, the sources said.....Estes, the sources said, told grand jurors that four men were involved in planning the murder of Marshall - Estes, Johnson troubleshooter and close aide Clifton C. Carter, triggerman Malcolm Everett (Mac) Wallace and Johnson himself. Estes is the only one of the four still alive....

The sources said Estes testified that he and Carter met at Estes' home in Pecos after Marshall's death and that Carter commented that Wallace "sure did botch it up."

The sources said Estes testified that Wallace planned to kill Marshall and make it look as if the death were suicide by carbon monoxide poisoning.

According to the sources, Estes testified that Wallace hit Marshall on the head and then placed a plastic bag over Marshall's head and the exhaust pipe of Marshall's pickup truck. About that time, the sources quoted Estes as saying, Wallace heard a noise that sounded like an approaching car. Fearing that he was about to be discovered, Wallace shot Marshall in the abdomen five times with the .22-caliber rifle and left the scene, the sources quoted Estes as testifying.

**"Before I was convicted,
Bobby Kennedy offered me a deal."**
-Billy Sol Estes

The following excerpt is from the June 23, 1996
Houston Chronicle article: "Last One Standing" by
Evan Moore -

It was no secret to many at the time that President John F. Kennedy and his brother, U.S. Attorney General Bobby Kennedy, detested Johnson and had not wanted him on the ticket but were forced to include him to ensure votes from Southern Democrats.

"My troubles just gave them a way out, they thought," says Estes.

Estes plight offered the Kennedys a no-fault opportunity to rid themselves of Johnson - if Johnson could be tied to the scandal surrounding the chubby millionaire from Pecos. They pursued Estes with a vengeance. Under the Kennedys, the FBI assigned 76 agents to investigate Estes. There were 16 federal auditors, and untold number of IRS agents, agents from the U.S. Attorney General's office, the Texas Attorney General's office and the Agriculture Department. By the winter of 1961, Pecos swarmed with agents ready to ply locals with liquor

"Before I was convicted, Bobby Kennedy offered me a deal."
-Billy Sol Estes

to find out anything about Billie Sol Estes.

A standing joke in Pecos in 1961 was that there was a shortage of margarine in town that winter because the FBI had circulated a memo advising that a grease-coated stomach would enable an agent to drink more.

"The unspoken word in the IRS was that our orders were to get Billie Sol Estes," says retired IRS investigator Ken Bradberry of San Angelo. "I've never thought Estes was lily-white or that he wasn't guilty of a lot of things, but he wasn't guilty of all the charges we eventually brought against him."

"Before I was convicted, Bobby Kennedy offered me a deal," says Estes. "He wanted me to turn evidence against Lyndon and they'd let me go free.

"I didn't take that deal. I'd have been free for 30 minutes. Then I'd have been dead. There were already some others who had gone that route." says Estes.

In the next two years, three other men with ties to Estes - George Krutilek, a Clint, Texas accountant; Amarillo businessman Harold Eugene Orr, and Chicago fertilizer supplier Howard Pratt - were found with indications that they had died of carbon monoxide poisoning, according to press reports at the time.

The sources close to the Robertson County grand jury said that Estes refused to answer questions about four deaths in West Texas, telling Dist. Atty. John Paschall that he wouldn't testify about anything "that would put me in the penitentiary." Paschall would not discuss the deaths Estes was asked about.

Sources close to the grand jurors said they considered part of Estes' testimony to be truthful but believed he was shading his story to put himself in a better light....

(end quotes)

Henry H. Marshall, reportedly refused a
Johnson-arranged promotion and transfer
to a post in Washington. It was then,
according to Billie Sol Estes' testimony,
that word was given to kill him.

The strange "suicide" of George Krutilek.

As the article "Last One Standing" (Houston Chronicle, June 23, 1996 - by Evan Moore) reports, there were some irregularities in the death of George Krutilek:

"Earlier, just four days after Estes was arrested, George Krutilek, 49, an El Paso accountant for the farmers who signed the ammonia-tank mortgages, had been found dead in his car near El Paso, a week before he was scheduled to give a deposition in the Estes case.

A hose was attached to the exhaust and run through a rear window, but former El Paso County Sheriff's Capt Freddie Bonnilla says there was something strange about Krutilek's body. The man was propped awkwardly behind the wheel "stiff as a board and straight as an arrow. He'd obviously been dead long enough for rigor mortis to set in before he was shoved behind the wheel of that car." Bonilla reopened the Krutilek case in 1984, but found only skimpy reports and no evidence. No carbon monoxide was found in Krutilek's lungs. The cause of death was listed as "cardiac arrest" and the manner ruled "suicide," a ruling Bonilla believes was obviously wrong."

One cannot but wonder, after reading this reported testimony, if Wallace was also responsible for the "carbon monoxide deaths" of others related to the Estes/Johnson affair. Clint Peoples himself remarked that the deaths of Krutilek, Orr and Pratt seemed too similar to be coincidence. "They were all carbon monoxide poisonings."

In examining the newspaper accounts of the 1962 grand jury investigation into the mysterious death of Henry Marshall, we found that the people of Texas were not the only ones following the bizarre case.

In an article concerning the 1962 investigation, written January 6, 1985, David Hanners relates *(Dallas Morning News)*:

Among those watching the grand jury proceedings was Barefoot Sanders, then U. S. Attorney in Dallas and now a federal judge. Former Texas attorney General Will Wilson said Sanders, who has declined repeated requests for interviews on the Estes case, was in constant communication with Justice Department officials, particularly with Robert Kennedy, the U. S. Attorney General. Wilson said he believed Kennedy, who Wilson said had an intense dislike for Johnson, had sent Sanders to monitor the grand jury to see if the Vice President's name arose.

Other sources seemed to agree with this scenario. It was generally known by many, that there was a political rift between Johnson and Robert Kennedy.

Hanners, in another article related to the 1962 event, dated April 4, 1984, says:

In his appearance before the grand jury last month, Estes testified that Robert Kennedy may have offered

Marshall protection if he would testify against Johnson, sources said.

Sources close to the grand jury said Estes testified that Johnson, while Senate majority leader, controlled a political "slush fund" raised from some of Estes' illegal business dealings.

"He (Sanders) made, several times daily, telephone reports to Robert Kennedy as to what was happening," Wilson said. "We were aware of the tremendous emotional and personal rivalry between Robert Kennedy and LBJ. The Kennedys closely observed the proceedings and followed them by the hour."....Wilson said he believes Estes is telling the truth about the plot.

We were fortunate to find a copy of *Clint Peoples — Texas Ranger*, at the library. In it we quickly found an account describing his investigation of the Marshall murder. We were impressed with his explanation of the facts surrounding the case. Surely, we could see that this had been a murder; a botched murder perhaps, but a murder nonetheless.

From *Clint Peoples - Texas Ranger*:

Over the years Clint Peoples has become an expert in homicide investigation. He has worked hard at understanding the processes by which one undertakes to scientifically gather and sift evidence leading to solving a murder case. There is some intuition involved in each case, but mostly it is just hard work. And it is with the hard work in mind that Peoples states that he has missed on "very, very few" murder cases in his half century in law enforcement. But according to his wife, the most perplexed he ever was on an investigation of any sort was the Henry H. Marshall case. "I'll go to my grave knowing Henry Marshall was murdered," Peoples says in acknowledging this, his most puzzling investigation, one of the "very, very few" he has not been able to solve.

Henry Marshall, age fifty-one, lived in Bryan with his wife and ten-year-old son Donald. He was employed by the Agricultural Stabilization and Conservation Committee of the United States Department of Agriculture, working out of College Station. His boss described him as a "highly respected and dedicated public servant" who had been offered higher positions in Washington which he had refused, preferring to live in Bryan. Marshall carried a heavy work load which had caused him to have a "health problem" and threatened to reduce his working capacity to half-time. Some persons close to him were aware that Marshall had a bed in or near his office where he rested every day, and he told his brother-in-law, L. M. Owens, that he had a knot in his back which might be cancer. Others believed he had a heart condition, but whatever health problem he had it was not of recent origin. Marshall had lived with it a long time.

Saturday, June 3, 1961 was a day off, which offered Marshall the opportunity to go out to his ranch in Robertson County to look around and do some work. This "place", as ranch or farm properties are sometimes called, was Marshall's hobby, his special interest, and he spent a lot of time at it. L. M. Owens worked for him on the place sometimes mending fences, seeing to crops and feeding the cattle. Owens noticed that Marshall recently had taken to driving in a back pasture where he looked over the feeder and talked quite a bit about it. It seemed a little unusual but Owens did not dwell on it. On June 3, Marshall stopped by the Owens house early before going thirteen miles northwest of Franklin to talk with Joe Pruitt and Wylie Grace, who with Lewis Taylor, were loading some hay on a truck. They were about ready to drive out of the Pruitt field when Marshall drove up in his Chevrolet pickup. Marshall gave Pruitt a $36 check for baling hay and he tried to pay Grace for cutting the hay, but Grace declined. They visited for about twenty minutes and then, by 8:00 am, Marshall was gone. He went to his ranch and was involved in his *normal activities and last seen at 10:30 a.m. by Jim and Martha Wood, a black couple who lived nearby. When he did not report home late in the afternoon, Mrs. Marshall called to get Owens to find him. Owens and Irving Bennett found him dead near the feeder at 6:30 pm.*

When Robertson County Sheriff Howard Stegall, Deputy E. P. (Sonny) Elliott, and Ranger O. L. Luther arrived later, they looked around and decided it was suicide. Marshall had been shot five times with his .22 caliber rifle, which was found near the body. Marshall's glasses, watch, and pencils had been removed from their places and were on the seat of the pickup along with a single edge razor blade. At a quick glance it looked like suicide, and that is what they called it. No one paid attention to the fact that the rifle had a bolt action, one which had to be worked every time the rifle was fired. The following morning, Sunday, with the greenery of Central Texas at its best in late Spring (really early Summer in this locale) and the birds flitting and twittering overhead, Deputy Elliott took Justice of the Peace Lee Farmer out to the scene. It looked like suicide to Farmer, so he recorded it as such in his official report. While there, Elliott picked up a spent .22 caliber cartridge casing.

Meanwhile the family gathered. From Denison about dawn on June 4 came Mrs. Marshall's sister and her two sons, nineteen-year-old Jackie Leroy Anderson and fifteen-year-old Jerry Wayne Anderson. They were naturally curious as they looked at Uncle Henry's pickup which had blood smeared on it in several places, on the right side near the door handle, on the hood and right rear fender and on the left door just below the door handle. They also saw a dent, six to eight inches in diameter, centered in the lower half of the right door. Owens and the Anderson boys drove out to Marshall's farm that morning and just out of curiosity, placed the pickup at the same place Owens had found it. They then looked around and found a raisin box and some cigarette butts which had been smoked down to the filter so they could not tell what kind they were. They picked up the filters and put them in the raisin box which got lost later. Owens convinced them that it was suicide, saying, "Remember, I know more about Henry Marshall than you think I do. I worked for him and was with him a lot." When they got back to Franklin, Owens asked the young men to wash the truck, and they did.

Henry Marshall was buried as the family returned to normalcy. Mrs. Marshall soon went to Lee Farmer to ask that the cause of death be changed from suicide, but Farmer thought he was right, so he stuck to it. That ended things. Ended them that is, until May, 1962, when Secretary of Agriculture Orville Freeman stated that Henry Marshall had been a "key figure" in the investigation of the affairs of Billie Sol Estes. The connection was cotton allotments. Estes found cotton farming to be profitable so he set out in 1960 to grow all he could. He discovered that the only obstacle to growing more cotton and making more money was that the federal government imposed strict acreage controls in exchange for its price supports on cotton. The acreage allotment remains with the land and it cannot otherwise be sold or exchanged. Once acreage allotment for cotton is set, it stays with the land and is sold with it. The only exception to the rule is on land taken away by the right of eminent domain. When this happened, then the allotment could be transferred to other land bought by the same person within three years. These transfers had to be approved by the Department of Agriculture, and in Texas they were screened at College Station by Henry Marshall. Estes saw the loophole in cotton allotments and went right to it. He persuaded farmers in Texas, Oklahoma, Georgia and Alabama who had lost cotton land by eminent domain to purchase land from him. The plan was for a farmer to buy the land, place the cotton allotment on it, and then lease it to Estes for $50 per acre. The farmer was to pay Estes for the land purchase in four installments, but it was understood in advance that the farmer would fail to make the first payment, after which Estes would foreclose. The final result was that Estes still had the land, only now it was an acreage upon which cotton could be grown. By June, 1961, Estes was already in trouble over his cotton allotments because agriculture officials were onto his scheme, and it is a coincidence that he started getting in trouble at the same time as Henry Marshall's death. Homer Garrison had the "coincidence" called to his attention, after which he decided that a closer look should be had. Garrison assigned Peoples to investigate. Taking Ranger Johnny Krumnow with him, Peoples began on May 10, 1962, and he made his report to Garrison on July 13. In between, Rangers Krumnow, Hendrichs, Luther, Horton, Wilson, Riddles, J. S. Nance and Glenn Elliott had questioned everybody connected or possibly connected with the death. Mrs. Marshall, L. M. Owens, Irving Bennett, and Bob Marshall, Henry Marshall's brother, had all taken polygraph tests which showed that they knew nothing of how Marshall had met his death.

By May 21 Peoples had enough evidence to convince District Judge John M. Barron and County Attorney Bryan Russ to call a grand jury "for the purpose of obtaining evidence regarding Marshall's death." Peoples was the first to present for all the proceedings so he could hear witnesses' testimony. Fifty-five witnesses testified in the five weeks of hearings. The grand jury was concerning itself with whether it was suicide or homicide, but Peoples was already convinced it was the latter and he was trying to decide who had done it. That afternoon, judge Barron ordered that the body be disinterred for autopsy. Peoples was there when they brought the casket out of the ground to be taken to the Callaway-Jones Funeral Home in Bryan.

Dr. Joseph A. Jachimczyk, the chief medical examiner for Harris County, was called to Bryan to do the autopsy. Jachimczyk was a veteran in his trade, a man who had worked with some 15,000 corpses, one who performed autopsies daily. He was assisted by Dr. Ray Cruse of Hearne and James L. Turner, an investigator from his own staff. In addition to Peoples, those present were Judge Barron, Sheriff Stegall, Fred R. Rymer, DPS ballistics expert Charles H. Beardsley, Cal Killingsworth, and Dr. James I. Lindsay. The vault was opened at 7:30 a.m., the body identified by Manley Jones, the embalmer of almost a year ago, and the examination of the body began at 8:30.

129

Jachimczyk was thorough in his work. He went through the body systematically looking at everything, describing the "thin layer of black mold, which scraped off fairly easily" and the "scalp which slipped readily off the calvarium upon touching." But such thing were incidental to the doctor's research. He wanted to know the cause of death. To this end he took ninety-seven specimens for examination.

His twelve-page report concluded that Marshall came to his death as a result of five gunshot wounds in the chest and abdomen. Three of the wounds were "rapidly incapacitating," while two would require a little more time. Marshall, he felt, could not have lived more that thirty minutes after he sustained the wounds. He found two further complicating factors. Marshall had a bruise on the left side of the head and he had a 15 per cent carbon monoxide saturation in the blood from the left chest cavity, which he said could have been as high as 30 per cent at the time of death. For the grand jury, the punch-line of the report was Jachimczyk's final conclusion: "Being familiar with bizarre gunshot injuries, one cannot say, however, on a purely scientific basis that a verdict of suicide is absolutely impossible in this case; most improbable, but not impossible." He pronounced it as a "possible suicide, probable homicide."

Dr. Jachimczyk telephoned his findings to Judge Barron on May 24 as the investigation proceeded. Peoples was in Austin the following day giving Garrison a briefing after which "The Boss" said to keep going. On May 29 and May 30 Peoples conferred with Judge Barron, County Attorney Russ and the grand jury, and he did it again on June 4. June 3, the first anniversary of Marshall's death, found him in the maelstrom of a mystery. After the grand jury had considered the evidence presented, they concluded on June 25 that there was no reason to change the verdict from suicide. Jury Foreman Goree Matthews did state that they agreed to come back into session at any time to hear additional evidence. County Attorney Bryan Russ agreed, stating that he had "no evidence to indicate that it was other than suicide." Sheriff Stegall was asked if he thought

Marshall could have worked the bolt on the rifle to reload after each shot, and he replied that he thought it possible. "I do know this," he continued, "a man can stand up under a lot of lead. A .22 does not have much shocking power...I saw a man hit four times once and walk off." Since that time the legal question of Marshall' death - suicide or murder - has not been opened.

For Peoples the case never stopped. He continued to have his Rangers follow every lead, doing the coordinating and analyzing himself. On July 13, 1962 he made an extensive report to Colonel Garrison, a part of which reads: Our investigation reveals that for Mr. Henry Marshall to have committed suicide the following acts would have had to occur:

[1] The first act of Mr. Marshall would have been to take carbon monoxide. (Pathologist's report reveals that 15% carbon monoxide was present at time of autopsy one year later and 15% would have been lost from embalming processes, a lethal dose consisting of 40%)

[2] Mr. Marshall would have had to dispose of the facilities with which the carbon monoxide was administered

[3] Mr. Marshall received a serious brain injury on the left side of his head from a fall and a cut over his left eye, causing the eye to protrude.

[4] Severe bruises with skin breakage on the back of his hands.

[5] Blood left on the right side of the pickup truck, also on rear and left side of pickup.

[6] Mr. Marshall would have had to cut off the motor on the pickup.

[7] Absence of blood inside of pickup after motor was cut off.

[8] Absence of blood on front of Mr. Marshall's shirt.

[9] Shirt of deceased was open with no bullet holes in front.

[10] Nitrites present only on tail of Mr. Marshall's shirt (back side).

[11] A deep dent present on right side of pickup caused by some type of instrument other than a human hand or head which was placed there on this date.

[12] Due to lack of blood on front of shirt but considerable blood present around pickup creates another mystery.

[13] Investigation revealed that it was difficult for Mr. Marshall to straighten out his right arm, which was due to a prior injury, and it would have been necessary for him to pull the trigger with his left hand.

After all of the above acts Mr. Henry Marshall would have had to have sufficient control of his equilibrium to have fired five bullets into the front of his left abdomen with a .22 bolt-action rifle, taking it down each time and ejecting the shell. The five bullets passing through Mr. Marshall's body traveled at a substantially straight angle which would indicate that he had to have extreme control of his equilibrium, after receiving all injuries from falls preceding the shooting of himself. From the direction of travel of bullets Mr. Marshall would have had entrance wounds which would have been more difficult. This fact was determined by the pattern of spent shells which were found by this Division and other parties after the death of Henry Marshall. Markers were placed by parties who found the spent shells at the time. Tests were made of the gun to establish a pattern of shell ejections which revealed that they were of a pattern identical to those found at the scene. Sand in the entire area was sifted; no bullets present. Mine detector was used; no other spent shells found.

A conclusion reached from this investigation is that had Mr. Henry Marshall shot himself before all of the acts above pointed out he would have had to return to where the empty shells were found and then collapse, which under the circumstances above mentioned would have been impossible for the following reasons: (1) Investigation reveals that there was no blood present on the ground other than where the body was found, (2) the only blood present on Henry Marshall's shirt was at the exit holes in the back and was a very small amount, (3) autopsy reveals that three of the shots were incapacitating, one severing the aorta and two paralyzing, and (4) autopsy report also reveals that the man died quickly from internal hemorrhaging.

It is a conclusion of this writer that Mr. Marshall did not live long after shots were fired into his body for the reason that so long as there is life in the body, the heart is pumping and so long as the heart is pumping, blood will flow from the exit of a gunshot wound. Reasonable deductions are that Mr. Marshall did not move from the location where the shots were fired into his body. It would have been impossible for him to have first fired the shots with such accuracy under the influence of carbon monoxide, secondly committed the acts above mentioned and return to the spot where the shells were found and died. It is reasonable to conclude that this would not have been possible for him to have returned and scuffed up the ground with his foot as indicated in a dying condition. Witnesses reveal that the ground was scuffed up with his foot where he was found lying.

An extensive investigation was conducted, as result of the suicidal ruling, to determine the reason for suicide motivation; no reason can be established. All reports reveal that Mr. Henry Marshall was a dedicated, honest and loyal government employee. Records also reveal that due to the vast operation of the cotton and grain program of Texas and Mr. Marshall's reluctance to approve many shady aspects he, without a doubt, created animosity among people who were attempting to accomplish their goals. From the findings of this investigation it is my personal opinion that it would have been beneficial to a vast number of shady operators for Mr. Henry Marshall to have been disposed of. It is my conclusion from the extensive investigation made by this department with the assistance of the scientific approach, evidence obtained, witnesses' testimonies, physical checks and tests made at the scene, it would have been utterly impossible for Mr. Marshall to have taken his own life.

Now we knew clearly what Madeleine Brown meant when she told us that "Wallace worked for Lyndon." Could this man's fierce loyalty to Johnson be the driving force that enabled him to commit murder? And if so, what was the reason for his loyalty?

Part of the answer lies in the death of John Kinser. Though some might find it hard to believe that Wallace was LBJ's "troubleshooter", history documents at least one murder that Wallace did commit. A murder that was likewise connected to Lyndon Johnson.

It is not precisely known what Wallace's motive was in killing John Kinser. Some say that Kinser, 33, was a man-about-town, who was having an affair with Malcolm's estranged wife. Others say that Malcolm Wallace was dating Josepha Johnson, LBJ's sister. There is speculation of a romantic rivalry between Wallace and Kinser, for the affections of Josepha, which led to the cold-blooded murder of Kinser on October 22, 1951.

Even though the motive is unclear, the facts of the murder seem to be well known. Wallace, according to the newspaper accounts, walked into the clubhouse at the Butler Pitch and Putt Golf Course in Austin, where Kinser worked. No one heard their short conversation, but several people heard the single "pop" from a .25 caliber pistol. Wallace was seen walking quickly from the scene with the gun in his hand. Even though the gun was never recovered, it was reported that Wallace was given the small caliber (.25 automatic) weapon years before, by an F.B.I. friend in Fort Worth.

Within an hour, Wallace was arrested nine miles from Austin. By strange coincidence, Clint Peoples was put in charge of the case. Working with Peoples was Detective Marion Lee. In a Dallas Times Herald article written by William P. Barrett, we found that the arresting officers heard Wallace say that he was working for "Mr. Johnson", and was anxious to get back to Washington. He was released on a $30,000 bond -later reduced to $10,000.

Detective Marion Lee, formerly with the Austin Police Department, said that when Wallace was arrested in 1951 on charges of killing John Douglas Kinser on an Austin golf course, Wallace told investigators "he was working for Mr. Johnson and (that's why) he had to get back to Washington."

At the time, Johnson was a U. S. senator and Wallace ostensibly was working as an economist for the U. S. Department of Agriculture. Still, said Lee, "He (Wallace) indicated to us that he worked in some office that was connected with Mr. Johnson."

In Clint People's book (*Clint Peoples - Texas Ranger*) he says this about the investigation:

"....there was an added dimension in that Wallace had friendly connections with Lyndon B. Johnson's family and with several high-ranking state officials. ....the smell of politics was all around there."

On November 18, 1951, Wallace was indicted for murder by the grand jury, and his ten day trial began February 18, 1952 in the 98th District Court of Travis County, with Judge Charles Betts presiding. Defending Wallace was none other than John Cofer and Polk Shelton, both with long-standing ties with Lyndon Johnson. Cofer had been legal counsel to LBJ in the legal maneuvering surrounding his questionable 1948 election to the U. S. senate. Strangely, it was also Cofer who "defended" Billie Sol Estes in his trial a decade later. The strange trial is described nicely in the J. Evetts Haley book: *A Texan Looks at Lyndon* in this way:

"The case went to trial. District Attorney Bob Long- notwithstanding the identity of the car, a bloody shirt and a cartridge of the same caliber as used in the shooting, found in Wallace's possession, and witnesses who heard the shots and saw the departure of a man who fit Wallace's description - described it as "a near perfect murder."

Wallace did not take the stand. No evidence was presented to suggest cause of extenuating circumstances. Cofer simply filed a brief, one-page motion for an instructed verdict, pleading that there was no evidence upon which the State could "legally base a judgment of guilt." Long said nothing whatever in rebuttal. After less than two hours of testimony which was shut off so "abruptly" that it "left the packed courtroom with jaws ajar." Long urged the jury to "punish Wallace in whatever degree you can agree upon."

Thus after one of the briefest and most perfunctory trials of a prominent murder case on record, even in Texas, the jury nonetheless found, March 27, 1952, (actually Feb.) that Wallace was, as charged, guilty "of murder with malice aforethought." Its penalty, a five-year suspended sentence - for murder in the first degree....

Wallace returned to his work in Washington and five years to a day later appeared back in the 98th District Court to have his record wiped clean, citizenship restored."

It is difficult, if not impossible, to read these accounts and not believe that Malcolm Wallace had friends in high places. Clint Peoples recounts that the prosecutor, Bob Long, had made the statement, "I lost it (the trial) because I let a sinker get on the jury."

A sinker is another word for "fixer," and rumors abounded in Austin for years that there had been a "fixer" on the jury to ensure that Wallace never served any time for the killing. But according to William Barrett, the rumor turned out to be true. In an article in *the Dallas Times Herald*, dated March 31, 1986, Barrett wrote:

One of the biggest mysteries in the Kinser killing is how the jury could convict Wallace of murder with malice, but recommend only a suspended sentence. In a recent Times Herald interview, juror D. L. Johnson, 68, a retired Highway Department employee, acknowledged he was the first cousin and good friend of Gus Lanier, who during the trial sat at the defense table of Wallace and his main lawyers.

D. L. Johnson, who is not related to LBJ, also said he alone among the jurors favored acquittal and that he forced the guilty-with-suspended-sentence verdict by threatening to cause a hung jury.

I was able to contact Mr. Barrett when I returned from Dallas. He confirmed the above information, and told me without hesitation that in his own mind, he is absolutely sure, beyond doubt, that Malcolm Wallace had the help of Lyndon Johnson in his legal battle.

Much later, we found *The Texas Observer* article (Nov. 7, 1986) by Bill Adler, which added further support to a "fixed" jury in the Wallace case:

"Not long after the trial, several of the jurors telephoned Doug Kinser's parents to apologize for voting for a suspended sentence, but said they did so only because threats had been made against their families, according to Al Kinser, a nephew of Kinser's who along with his father, still runs the Pitch and Putt golf course."

We were pleased with the way our research was taking shape. Mark and I had decided from the beginning to follow every possible lead and let the story unfold by itself. We would not force it into a preconceived mold, but rather, follow it to its logical and obvious conclusion. When we started looking into Loy's story, we had no notions or preconceptions of where it would lead. And so here we were, reading and absorbing information about Malcolm Wallace, a man that would have remained nameless and obscure, had it not been for the courage of Loy Factor.

We discovered, in the Dallas County Library, the yearbooks of the University of Texas at Austin. In them, we were able to copy several excellent photographs of Malcolm Wallace. These we would enlarge and in due time bring them to Loy to examine. Was this the same man who met Loy at the 1961 funeral of Sam Rayburn? Was this the same man who was responsible for the death of President Kennedy? We felt that we knew the answer; but we now needed to prove it.

We left the library late in the afternoon, content with the information we had found. We had much more to look at, which we planned on doing the next day, but we were anxious to get back to our hotel, and our appointment with Madeleine Brown.

Chapter 12
The Incredible Ms. Madeleine Brown

If it weren't for Madeleine Brown, we would still be looking for the mysterious "Wallace", who not only hired the killers of President Kennedy, but fired one of the shots himself. Loy Factor may have been our key, but it was Madeleine who turned the key.

We had spent much time with this Texas legend on the telephone, but when she walked into the meeting room on the 28th floor of the Southwest Hotel Tower in Dallas, we finally got to meet face to face for the first time. She was equally as curious about us. She had been stunned when Larry Howard phoned her and informed her of our interview with Loy Factor and his naming Wallace as the mastermind of the conspiracy. Madeleine saw for the first time a chance to corroborate her many suspicions about Malcolm Wallace.

She immediately became comfortable with us. We had already heard much of her knowledge of Wallace, but we wanted to hear it in person. In addition to allowing us to tape record an interview with her, she was generous enough to bring along her (then) unpublished manuscript- *"Texas In The Morning"*, detailing her 20 year affair with Lyndon Johnson. "Billie Sol says its the dirtiest book he's ever read, but I think it will give you the background that you need for your story," Madeleine said, handing the huge manuscript to me. It was replete with pictures of the wild Texas era that she thrived in for decades.

She openly states in her book that Johnson had made a veiled threat that Kennedy was going to be killed:

On Thursday night, Nov. 21, 1963, the last evening prior to Camelot's demise, I attended a social at Clint Murchison's home. It was my understanding that the event was scheduled as a tribute honoring his long time friend, J. Edgar Hoover (whom Murchison had first met decades earlier through President William Howard Taft), and his companion, Clyde Tolson. Val Imm, the society editor for the now-defunct Dallas Times Herald, unwittingly documented one of the most significant gatherings in American history. The impressive guest list included John McCloy, Richard Nixon, George Brown, R. L. Thornton, H. L. Hunt and a host of others from the 8F group. The jovial party was just breaking up when Lyndon made an unscheduled visit. I was the most surprised by his appearance since Jesse had not mentioned anything about Lyndon's coming to Clint's. With Lyndon's hectic schedule, I never dreamed he could attend the big party. After all, he had arrived in Dallas on Tuesday to attend the Pepsi-Cola convention. Tension filled the room upon his arrival. The group immediately went behind closed doors. A short time later Lyndon, anxious and red-faced, re-appeared.

I knew how secretly Lyndon operated. Therefore I said nothing... not even that I was happy to see him. Squeezing my hand so hard, it felt crushed from the pressure, he spoke with a grating whisper, a quiet growl, into my ear, not a love message, but one I'll always remember: "After tomorrow those goddamn Kennedys will never embarrass me again - that's no threat - that's a promise."

The next morning (November 22, 1963) Madeleine tells of another brief discussion that she had with Lyndon:

I had barely eked out the words, "About last night..." when his rage virtually went ballistic. His snarling voice jolted me as never before - "That son-of-a-b---- crazy Yarborough and that g- - - - - - f - - - ing Irish mafia bastard Kennedy will never embarrass me again!"

Madeleine has stuck by her story for many years and continues to this day to say that Lyndon Johnson knew what was coming and when.

We asked if she had made any references to Wallace in her book.

"Oh yes, he appears in various places throughout the manuscript," she replied.

She scanned through a few pages and picked one out, reading it aloud to us from page 84:

"....Malcolm E. Wallace, a former University of Texas student body president who was working as an economist for the Dept. of Agriculture. He was generally known as "Lyndon's boy" (a hatchet man like Jesse Kellam)."

Then another quotation from page 90:

"Malcolm E. Wallace .... who left a trail of bloody murders. To many of us he is still a prime suspect in President Kennedy's assassination. I had met with U. S. Marshall Clint Peoples to discuss Malcolm Wallace because I had

witnessed Mac practicing at the Dallas Gun Club. Clint had investigated Wallace's death for years. He was planning to break the case open, with proof that Wallace was one of the shooters behind the picket fence overlooking Dealey Plaza. Unfortunately Clint's untimely death in mysterious circumstances prevented this announcement from ever being made....

"We found it extremely significant that this had been written by Madeleine over a year before we made contact and interviewed Loy Factor.

"With my hand to god," Madeleine said to us, while holding up her right hand, "I have always felt that Mac Wallace was one of the gunmen in Dealey Plaza that day. Billie Sol does too, but he doesn't want to talk about it. I think he knows a lot more than he lets on - and Clint Peoples was convinced of it too."

On more than one occasion, she had seen Malcolm Wallace in the company of LBJ. Once, she had caught a glimpse of Johnson, Wallace, Cliff Carter, Jerome Ragsdale, and Jesse Kellam together in the executive offices of the Johnson broadcast station KTBC in Austin. Wallace, it appeared to Madeleine, was a very low-profile part of Lyndon Johnson's team.

She was very convinced that Loy Factor was telling the truth about his involvement with Wallace and the other conspirators, especially when she heard of the circumstances of Loy meeting Wallace at the Rayburn funeral. She explained that Wallace moved in the same circles with Johnson, Sam Rayburn, Amon Carter, Cliff Carter, H. L. Hunt and Clint Murchison, to name but a few. It would not be surprising that Wallace would attend the funeral of LBJ's good friend and mentor, Sam Rayburn - it would be a perfectly natural place for him to be. (Later, Madeleine, in a conversation with Billie Sol Estes, would be told that Wallace and Billie Sol were together at the 1961 funeral of Sam Rayburn.)

Madeleine was also impressed when we told her about Jack Ruby, as she had known Ruby for several years, and used to frequent his club. We recounted Loy's story about Ruby becoming extremely concerned that the motorcade route had been changed, a day or so before the assassination, and then Ruth Ann leaving to check out the rumor. Madeleine told us of her association with Ruby.

"We used to go to his club once in a while and drink ol' Southern peach brandys. You know, the kind that really warm you up on a cold evening! Well Jack was always glad to see us. He always referred to us as 'you classy guys.' One night, at the Carousel Club, about a week and a half before the assassination, Jack comes over to where I'm sitting with Larry Buchanan, the creative director for our ad agency. He has a map of the presidential motorcade route in his hand and he proceeds to show it off to us."

"He had a map of the motorcade route?" Mark asked.

"He sure did. We always knew that Jack had all the inside scoop on everything that went on in Dallas. He knew everyone in the police department, and we knew he had connections with the mob too. We used to call him P. C. - for privileged character."

"What did he say about the motorcade map?"

"Well, I asked him how in the hell did he get that
kind of information, but he just smiled, and never
answered us directly. It was his way of showing off
... you know, letting us know that he had
connections."

The extent of Jack Ruby's participation in the
assassination may never be known beyond what we know
from these witnesses. He obtained inside information about
the president's motorcade route, and he apparently drove
Oswald to the house to meet with Wallace, Loy and the
others. Madeleine knew of several who had seen Oswald at
Ruby's club. And as it was dramatically pointed out to us
on an earlier Dallas trip, Oswald had been stopped by
Officer J. D. Tippit halfway between Oswald's rooming
house and Jack Ruby's apartment. To many, it appears that
Oswald was heading directly to Ruby's. As for Ruby killing
Oswald in jail, this again would be attributable to his
"insider" status with the Dallas Police Department. Thus,
Ruby's ability to gather sensitive information, and his
relationship with Dallas authorities made him a useful part
of Wallace's team. One can only guess that Ruby, at
Wallace's order, was covering up for the group with the
hope that he, like Malcolm Wallace in 1952, would be
cleared of charges and soon be a free man. He was
scheduled for a retrial in 1967, but died of cancer before it
could happen. We can only speculate about what the
verdict would have been had he lived to face a new trial.

Perhaps one of Ruby's comments to Al Maddox, his
jailer, can be better understood in the light of the above:
"In order to understand the assassination," Ruby said, "you
have to read the book *A Texan Looks at Lyndon*." Of course
it is in the above referenced book that the author not only
assails Lyndon Johnson's character, but also details the
murder of John Kinser, along with the arrest and strange
trial of Malcolm Everett Wallace!

Madeleine attempted to arrange an interview with Billie Sol Estes for us but was unable to contact him. She provided us with his phone number and said that she would tell him to expect a call from us when we returned home from Texas. I called Estes some days later and talked with him at great length, but was unable to elicit any information concerning his relationship with Wallace or LBJ. His only reply was, "I just don't talk about those days anymore." He was very kind, but not at all helpful.

We concluded our interview of Madeleine Brown with a very strong feeling, one that continues to this very day - that individuals like her and Billie Sol Estes need to be given closer attention. They hold much information that needs to be examined and scrutinized. Especially Estes, who fears to talk to anyone without the protection of immunity. He has spent many years in prison and dreads the thought of returning there in his golden years. He has hinted in various interviews that maybe someday this will change. To David Hanners of *the Dallas Morning News*, Estes said:

> *"I think history will be put straight someday - I think it will."*

It is the hope of these writers that the day will come soon.

Chapter 13
The Estes Documents

The 1984 grand jury testimony of Billie Sol Estes accomplished only one official action. Henry Marshall's death certificate was finally changed to read: "Cause of death - murder by gunshot." But at the same time, the proceedings attracted the attention of the United States Justice Department. Estes received an official letter requesting a meeting to discuss the provocative charges he had made before the grand jury. Estes enlisted the legal services of Douglas Caddy to represent him in this matter. Caddy corresponded with the Justice Department in an attempt to secure the protection of immunity from prosecution for his client. A few months after the release of *"The Men On The Sixth Floor"*, I received two of these letters of negotiation between Estes and the Justice Department. We made these letters public by including them in the second edition of our book, and now we include the remaining two letters that have made their way to us in this, our updated edition. None of these documents have been previously available prior to their publication by us. Because they reflect the sensitive negotiations between the government and a private citizen, it is unlikely they would ever have become public, had it not been for certain sources who, after reading the first version of our book, were compelled to send this information to us.

146

We now present all four letters, the complete record of correspondence between Billie Sol Estes and the United States Justice Department.

Letter #1:

May 29, 1984

U. S. Justice Department
Criminal Division

Douglas Caddy
Attorney-at-Law
General Homes Building
7322 Southwest Freeway
Suite 610
Houston, Texas 77074

Dear Mr. Caddy:

RE: Billy Sol Estes

I have considered the materials and information you have provided to me in connection with your representation of Billy Sol Estes. I understand that Mr. Estes claims to have information concerning the possible commission of criminal offenses in Texas in the 1960's and that he is willing to reveal that information at this time. I also understand that Mr. Estes wants several things in exchange for this information, such as a pardon for the offenses for which he has been convicted and immunity from any further prosecution among other things. Before we can engage in any further discussions concerning Mr. Estes' cooperation or enter into any agreement with Mr. Estes we must know the following things: (1) the information, including the extent of corroborative evidence, that Mr. Estes has about each of the events that may be violations of criminal law; (2) the sources of his information; and (3) the extent of his involvement, if any, in each of those events or any subsequent cover-ups. Until we have detailed information concerning these three things we can not determine whether any violations of federal criminal law occurred which are within our jurisdiction to investigate and prosecute and, if so, whether the information is credible and otherwise warrants investigation. Accordingly, if we are to proceed with meaningful discussions concerning Mr. Estes' proffered cooperation, we must receive a detailed and specific written offer of proof from you setting forth the information noted above. The government will hold your offer of proof in strictest confidence and will not make any use of it other than to determine the credibility of the proffered information and whether it warrants further discussions with or debriefings of Mr. Estes.

I must make sure that several things are understood at this time concerning Mr. Estes' proffered cooperation. First, if after reviewing your offer of proof we decide the information that Mr. Estes can provide is credible and in all other respects warrants further investigation -- a decision which will be made unilaterally by the government -- it will be necessary for Mr. Estes to be interviewed and to reveal everything he knows about the possible criminal violations. He will have to do so completely, truthfully and without guile. Second, it must be understood that the government is not now making specific promises to Mr. Estes except with respect to the confidentiality and use of your offer of proof as noted above. If it is decided that Mr. Estes should be interviewed, the extent of promises concerning the confidentiality or use of the statement or promises of reward or consideration to Mr. Estes, if any, will be determined only after we receive a detailed written offer of proof from you.

Above all else, I must emphasize that Mr. Estes must act with total honesty and candor in any dealings with the Department of Justice or any investigative agency. If any discussions with or debriefings of Mr. Estes take place after receipt of your offer of proof and if any agreement ultimately is reached after Mr. Estes provides a statement, the government will not be bound by any representations or agreements it makes if any of his statements at any time are false, misleading or materially incomplete or if he knowingly fails to act with total honesty and candor.

Sincerely

Stephen S. Trott

Assistant Attorney General

CriminalDivision

Letter #2

August 9, 1984

Mr. Stephen S. Trott
Assistant Attorney General,
Criminal Division
U.S. Department of Justice
Washington, D. C. 20530

RE: Mr. Billie Sol Estes

Dear Mr. Trott:

My client, Mr. Estes, has authorized me to make this reply to your letter of May 29, 1984.

Mr. Estes was a member of a four-member group, headed by Lyndon Johnson, which committed criminal acts in Texas in the 1960's. The other two, besides Mr. Estes and LBJ, were Cliff Carter and Mack Wallace.

Mr. Estes is willing to disclose his knowledge concerning the following criminal offenses:

I. Murders

1. The killing of Henry Marshall

2. The killing of George Krutilek

3. The killing of Ike Rogers and his secretary

4. The killing of Harold Orr

5. The killing of Coleman Wade

6. The killing of Josefa Johnson

7. The killing of John Kinser

8. The killing of President J. F. Kennedy.

Mr. Estes is willing to testify that LBJ ordered these killings, and that he transmitted his orders through Cliff Carter to Mack (Mac) Wallace, who executed the murders. In the cases of murders nos. 1-7, Mr. Estes' knowledge of the precise details concerning the way the murders were executed stems from conversations he had shortly after each event with Cliff Carter and Mack Wallace.

In addition, a short time after Mr. Estes was released from prison in 1971, he met with Cliff Carter and they reminisced about what had occurred in the past, including the murders. During their conversation, Carter orally compiled a list of 17 murders which had been committed, some of which Mr. Estes was unfamiliar. A living witness was present at that meeting and should be willing to testify about it. He is Kyle Brown, recently of Houston and now living in Brady, Texas.

Mr. Estes, states that Mack Wallace, whom he describes as a "stone killer" with a communist background, recruited Jack Ruby, who in turn recruited Lee Harvey Oswald. Mr. Estes says that Cliff Carter told him that Mack Wallace fired a shot from the grassy knoll in Dallas, which hit JFK from the front during the assassination.

Mr. Estes declares that Cliff Carter told him the day Kennedy was killed, Fidel Castro also was supposed to be assassinated and that Robert Kennedy, awaiting word of Castro's death, instead received news of his brother's killing.

Mr. Estes says that the Mafia did not participate in the Kennedy assassination but that its possible participation was discussed prior to the event, but rejected by LBJ, who believed if the Mafia were involved, he would never be out from under its blackmail.

Mr. Estes asserts that Mr. Ronnie Clark, of Wichita, Kansas, has attempted on several occasions to engage him in conversation. Mr. Clark, who is a frequent visitor to Las Vegas, has indicated in these conversations a detailed knowledge corresponding to Mr. Estes' knowledge of the JFK assassination. Mr. Clark claims to have met with Mr. Jack Ruby a few days prior to the assassination, at which time Kennedy's planned murder was discussed.

Mr. Estes declares that discussions were had with Jimmy Hoffa concerning having his aide, Larry Cabell, kill Robert Kennedy while the latter drove around in his convertible.

Mr. Estes has records of his phone calls during the relevant years to key persons mentioned in the foregoing account.

II. The Illegal Cotton Allotments

Mr. Estes desires to discuss the infamous illegal cotton allotment schemes in great detail. He has tape recordings made at the time of LBJ, Cliff Carter and himself discussing the scheme. These recordings were made with Cliff Carter's knowledge as a means of Carter and Estes protecting themselves should LBJ order their deaths.

Mr. Estes believes these tape recordings and the rumors of other recordings allegedly in his possession are the reason he has not been murdered.

III. Illegal Payoffs

Mr. Estes is willing to disclose illegal payoff schemes, in which he collected and passed on to Cliff Carter and LBJ millions of dollars. Mr. Estes collected payoff money on more than one occasion from George and Herman Brown of Brown and Root, which was delivered to LBJ.

In your letter of May 29, 1984, you request "(1) the information, including the extent of corroborative evidence, that Mr. Estes has about each of the events that may be violations of criminal law; (2) the sources of his information, and (3) the extent of his involvement, if any, in each of those events or any subsequent cover-ups."

In connection with Item # 1, I wish to declare, as Mr. Estes' attorney, that Mr. Estes is prepared without reservation to provide all the information he has. Most of the information contained in this letter I obtained from him yesterday for the first time. While Mr. Estes has been pre-occupied by this knowledge almost every day for the last 22 years, it was not until we began talking yesterday that he could face up to disclosing it to another person. My impression from our conversation yesterday is that Mr. Estes, in the proper setting, will be able to recall and orally recount a vast and detailed body of information about these criminal matters. It is also my impression that his interrogation in such a setting will elicit additional corroborative evidence as his memory is stimulated.

In connection with your Item #2, Mr. Estes has attempted in this letter to provide his sources of information.

In connection with your Item #3, Mr. Estes states that he never participated in any of the murders. It may be alleged that he participated in subsequent cover-ups. His response to this is that had he conducted himself any differently, he, too, would have been a murder victim.

Mr. Estes wishes to confirm that he will abide by the conditions set forth in your letter and that he plans to act with total honesty and candor in any dealings with the Department of Justice or any federal investigative agency.

In return for his cooperation, Mr. Estes wishes in exchange his being given immunity, his parole restrictions being lifted and favorable consideration being given to recommending his long-standing tax liens being removed and his obtaining a pardon.

Sincerely yours,

Douglas Caddy

Letter #3

Sept. 13, 1984

U. S. Department of Justice
Stephen S. Trott
Criminal Division

Douglas Caddy, Esquire
Attorney at Law
General Homes Building
7322 Southwest Freeway
Suite 610
Houston, Texas 77074

Re: Billie Sol Estes

Dear Mr. Caddy:

I have received your letter setting forth the specific allegations of Mr. Estes concerning the possible commission of criminal offenses in Texas in the 1960's. While no opinions or conclusions can be drawn at this time concerning the credibility of Mr. Estes' allegations, it is apparent that a detailed debriefing of Mr. Estes concerning these allegations is warranted. Therefore, if Mr. Estes still desires to provide information and evidence supporting his allegations, it is necessary for him to agree to a detailed interview by agents of the Federal Bureau of Investigation. He must further agree to the following:

1)   To submit to the interview under such circumstances as the government deems appropriate, including the use of a polygraph, in order for the FBI to be able to evaluate the credibility of Mr. Estes' allegations;

2)   to provide any and all information he has and any and all evidence in his possession or of which he has knowledge concerning the matters set forth in your letter of August 9, 1984, and not to withhold any information or evidence concerning such matters;

3)   to provide any and all information he has and any and all evidence in his possession or of which he has knowledge concerning any other alleged criminal conduct which the FBI may consider to be relevant in assessing the credibility of the information which is at the core of this process;

4) to provide all such information completely and truthfully and to act with total honesty and candor at all times, omitting nothing of which he has knowledge that is relevant in this inquiry.

You have represented that with regard to the alleged murders, Mr. Estes represents that he never participated in any of the killings.   If this representation is true and if Mr. Estes fully meets each of the requirements above, nothing said or revealed by Mr. Estes in the course of this interview will be used against him in a court of law.   If the representation is not true, the government will be free to use this information against him as well as any leads derived there from.

Mr. Estes has asked for other specific consideration in return for the information which he says that he possesses. Whether additional consideration will be extended to Mr. Estes and the nature and extent of any such consideration will be reviewed, considered and decided by the government after Mr. Estes has been interviewed. This decision will be made based upon our evaluation of the completeness and truthfulness of Mr. Estes' cooperation and the value and credibility of the information and evidence he provides. At the present time, Mr. Estes will submit to the proposed interview with no promises of any consideration whatsoever other than that nothing he says will be used against him in a court of law if he reveals the complete truth about what he knows.

I must emphasize that if Mr. Estes agrees to the conditions set forth in this letter, his obligation is to do nothing other than to candidly reveal the whole truth about the alleged criminal conduct. At all times, he shall tell the truth and nothing but the truth. Should any of his statements be false, misleading or materially incomplete or should he knowingly fail to act with total honesty and candor, the promise not to use any statements against Mr. Estes will be null and void and the government will not be bound by any other representations or agreements it makes. Furthermore, any knowing or reckless untruthful statement itself may be the predicate for criminal charges against Mr. Estes if it appears that he has provided false information which implicates an innocent person in the commission of a crime or perjures himself while under oath or makes false statements to the FBI or otherwise violates any statute in knowingly making such untrue statements.

One final comment is in order. The government is aware that general public discussion of allegations of criminal conduct can have an adverse affect upon not only the investigation of the allegations but also the reputations of those implicated. This is particularly true with respect to the present matter given the nature of the allegations and the fact that they concern persons who are not able to respond to them. Therefore, we believe it is particularly important in this matter, as in any other criminal matter, to maintain the utmost confidentiality conditions have been entered into other that these set forth in this letter and none will concerning these allegations.

No additional promises, agreements and be entered into unless in writing and signed by all parties.

Sincerely,

Stephen S. Trott

Assistant Attorney General

Criminal Division

Agreed and consented to:

_____

BILLIE SOL ESTES

_____

ATTORNEY FOR BILLIE SOL ESTES

In an interview with Mr. Lyle Sardie, an independent film-maker and researcher, Douglas Caddy explained some of the circumstances of the time.

Stephen Trott, an Assistant Attorney General with the Justice Department, went directly to William Sessions, then director of the FBI, to get permission to follow up on the Estes matter. Sessions gave him full permission, and assigned three young, energetic investigators to assist. An effort was made to assign agents who were young and not familiar with the Kennedy Assassination or the history of Billie Sol Estes. It was thought that they would be unbiased and fresh in their approach to the case. They opened the files on Estes and the Kennedy assassination and determined that an interview with Estes was necessary. In fact, the young agents were very excited at the possibilities.

Flying from Washington D.C. to Texas for their appointment to interview Estes, the FBI agents were met with a surprise when they met Billie Sol for breakfast, according to Caddy. Estes announced to the agents and Caddy, that he had decided not to go forward with the interview - and walked away. The agents, Caddy, and Billie Sol's daughter were shocked. No reason was ever given for the aborted session.

History still waits for the day when Estes will tell the full and truthful story of his relationship with Lyndon Johnson and the criminal activities they engaged in.

The Justice Department dispatched a final, bitter letter to Caddy and Estes. In it you can feel the frustration of having dealt with the "King of the Wheeler Dealers" - Billie Sol Estes.

Letter #4 - Final letter from Justice Department:

Nov. 1, 1984

U. S. Department of Justice
Stephen S. Trott
Criminal Division

Douglas Caddy, Esquire
Attorney at Law
General Homes Building
7322 Southwest Freeway
Suite 610
Houston, Texas 77074

    Re: Billie Sol Estes

Dear Mr. Caddy:

    I have been informed by the Federal Bureau of Investigation -- which undertook to interview Mr. Estes at my request based upon your offer of proof and representation that Mr. Estes desired to cooperate under the terms set forth in my September 13, 1984, letter to you -- that Mr. Estes refused to be interviewed by two agents who spent numerous hours reviewing Bureau files and who traveled to Abilene, Texas, from Washington for the sole purpose of interviewing Mr. Estes. Inasmuch as Mr. Estes is unable or unwilling to agree to completely and truthfully reveal to us the information he has -- which was the only condition required of him under my letter of September 13 -- we have closed the preliminary investigation of the allegations of Mr. Estes. We are compelled to close this matter not only because there simply is no credible evidence of any federal criminal offense, but also because of our promise to you in my letter of May 29, 1984, that we would not use your offer of proof except to make a decision as to whether we should interview Mr. Estes.

It must be evident to you and Mr. Estes that we do not take lightly allegations such as he made. The preliminary investigation of his allegations necessitated a substantial re-direction of resources of both the FBI and the Department from other serious matters. While we have promised not to make any use of the information revealed in your offer of proof, it would be wise for Mr. Estes to remember that he is on parole, and if he continues to make allegations which he is unwilling or unable to support, it is a matter which we will report to his probation officer.

Very truly yours,

Stephen S. Trott

Assistant Attorney General

The importance of these documents is obvious. Like the tip of an iceberg, they show a glimpse of what lies silent, below the surface. Unfortunately, the tip was all that the Justice Department and the FBI were to see. This is the way it has remained since 1984.

In early 1998, Lyle Sardie, was able to contact Kyle Brown, mentioned in the Estes letters as a witness to some of Estes' activities.   Sardie specifically asked Brown about the tapes that Estes purportedly had in his possession - tapes made of LBJ, without his knowledge.   Brown acknowledged the existence of these tapes and said that he had heard them in their entirety.   When asked about the content of the tapes, Brown reported:

"They prove that LBJ was a cold-blooded   killer, but then- we already knew that."

Later, Sardie told us that in 1998, a group of investors attempted to buy these tapes from Mr. Estes.   A cash offer of 1.5 million dollars was soundly turned down.

Do these tapes exist?   Many, including Mark and myself, think that they do.   Estes views these tapes as the means of his survival for the past three decades, and what he plans to do with them is anyone's guess.   One thing is certain however, - time and Billie Sol's health are slipping away.

The aborted 1984 interview needs to be renegotiated and carried out, along with the complete release of Estes' tapes, phone records and documents. Only then will a complete picture of the assassination and its architects emerge.

Chapter 14
On the Trail of Wallace

While in Texas, it was back to the seventh floor of the Dallas County Library to continue our search for information related to Malcolm Wallace. Since we had been inundated with information from files relating the Billie Sol Estes affair, we needed to finish weeding through it. It was like returning to a vein of gold - we knew it was rich, we just didn't know how much there was or how deep it would take us.

By the end of this second day we were able to determine, somewhat hazily, the career of Malcolm Wallace. We had already determined that he had attended the University of Texas in 1943-1947, and was elected as Student Body President in 1944. (We also should point out at this point that the man considered one of Lee Oswald's best friends, George DeMohrenschildt, also attended the University of Texas in 1944 to attain a degree in oil geology. Could Wallace and DeMohrenschildt have met then?)

Wallace also showed his proclivity towards political activism while at the University. In a *Dallas Morning News* article, dated March 29, 1984, we read:

In 1944, Malcolm Wallace was elected student government president at the University of Texas at Austin in a race that placed him against a fraternity-backed candidate. He was elected on a platform that promised greater academic freedom. While president, he led a march of university students on the state Capitol after the UT Board of Regents fired Dr. Homer P. Rainey as president. "He was one of the first people in Texas, one of the first Southern-bred people, to associate with blacks," Jerry Wallace (his brother) said.

The University of Texas yearbooks of those (1943-7) years show Wallace to be active in various clubs, including an organization of service veteran students, having served in the Marine Corps in 1939 and 1940, but discharged because of a back injury.

Wallace's classmates and friends while at the University of Texas are most interesting, in that they are, for the most part, closely connected to Lyndon Johnson. For example, in 1947, Professor Robert H. Montgomery (Dr. Bob) was one of Wallace's thesis advisors. He was, like U.T. President Homer Rainey, a controversial figure - one that the board of regents at the time wanted to fire. Apparently he was a bit "too liberal" for the board, but nevertheless very popular with the students. Montgomery had, during the war, worked with the O.S.S. - (later to become the CIA) in selecting "economic" bombing targets in Europe. In other words, the group was responsible for determining which targets would most severely affect the enemy's economy - be it oil, railroads and infrastructure, or manufacturing facilities. Part of this group earned the nickname "oily boys", for their predisposition towards blowing up oil facilities. Dr. Bob was also a close personal friend of LBJ, for in the 1930's young Lyndon lived in Montgomery's home for a period of time, according to a January, 1986 *Texas Monthly* article.

Another of Wallace's classmates, Horace Busby, later went on to become an advisor and speech writer for LBJ. Busby and Wallace were both members of the prestigious Friars Organization which consisted of only eight outstanding male class members each year. Busby was the editor of the *"Daily Texan"*, the UT newspaper that was widely read by many, including Texas politicians. Busby wrote several scathing articles in defense of University President Homer Rainey. It was Wallace who led the march on the state capitol in protest of Rainey's firing. According to author Eric F. Goldman in *The Tragedy of Lyndon Johnson:*

"Horace Busby....was considered so much the campus heretic that the university's minuscule Communist cell tried to recruit him. "

Quite likely it was from this period of time and these circumstances that led many to view Wallace himself as a Communist.

Then, there is Jack Brooks. Jack Bascom Brooks - was editor of *The Daily Texan* (UT newspaper), *The Cactus* (UT yearbook), member of numerous organizations at the University of Texas in 1943, his senior year. He, along with Wallace was also a member of MICA (Men's Inter-Community Association) of which Malcolm Wallace was Secretary-Treasurer according to page 245 of the 1943 Cactus yearbook) and Brooks was one of the men on the executive council. Brooks went on to become a Congressman, and as pointed out by Dallas researcher Larry Chenault, can be seen in the famous photo aboard Air Force One during the administering of the oath of office. He is standing behind and to the right of Mrs. Kennedy.

Aboard Air Force one before swearing in ceremony

Cliff Carter & LBJ at White House

Something we need no longer speculate about is the question of Wallace's ability to speak Spanish. As the reader will recall, Wallace first approached Factor at Sam Rayburn's funeral, speaking to the Indian in Spanish. In addition to Wallace, it was Factor's testimony that Ruth Ann and another young male Latin with her also conversed in Spanish. Larry Vaughn, another Austin researcher, has recently done an extensive search of Wallace's school records at the University of Texas. Among other things, Vaughn found a record of Wallace receiving a 'B' grade in "Spanish Reading & Comprehension," as well as documentation of his enrollment in a class known as "Economics of Spanish Speaking Countries of South America," which was taught by Eastin Nelson. He received an 'A' in that class. Wallace was also a member of the "Spanish Club" while a student at Woodrow Wilson High School. This information, coupled with the fact that many Texans are conversant in the Spanish language, lends credence to Loy Factor's claim that Wallace communicated with his Latin confederates in Spanish.

After Wallace graduated from the University of Texas, records reveal he studied at Columbia University in New York, then went to work in Washington D.C. as an economist for the U. S. Department of Agriculture. He married the former Mary Andre Barton in 1947, but three years later, in 1950, she filed for divorce. A year later Wallace was arrested for the first degree murder of John Douglas Kinser. Three months after his suspended sentence ruling, Wallace somehow managed to secure a job with the Temco company of Dallas, Texas. Temco, an acronym for the Texas Engineering and Manufacturing company, was a military aircraft plant, specializing in rebuilding aircraft, building aircraft sub-assemblies and similar projects. In 1959 the company was bought by Ling-Altec to form Ling-Temco, the predecessor of LTV. (Ling, Temco, Vought) According to company records, Wallace temporarily left Temco on November 21, 1952 and rejoined the company again on June 1, 1954, staying on for seven years, leaving February 19, 1961. His date of leaving Temco was three and a half months before Henry Marshall's murder.

During those years, Wallace held supervisory jobs in manufacturing control and long-range programming. The company held a variety of defense contracts, including those for the Navy's Corvus missile and the TT-1 Pinto Navy jet trainer. From 1959-61, Wallace was a general supervisor in program management for the Corvus missile contract. It is inconceivable, according to company spokespersons, that Wallace could have operated in these spheres without a security clearance. In fact, files showed that he did indeed have clearance right up until September 18, 1964, when the Defense Department's Industrial Personnel Access Authorization Screening Board stripped Wallace of the clearance on grounds of "criminal, infamous, immoral and notoriously disgraceful conduct." The reasons stated were: the murder conviction, two drunken driving convictions, indications that Wallace was a communist, as well as a homosexual. A portion of Wallace's Naval intelligence file states:

The FBI, San Antonio, Texas, had conducted a security type investigation of SUBJECT consequent to information received that SUBJECT was suspected of subversive affiliation with "common sense" groups and the 18 year-old movement (for voting franchise) believed to be a possible front organization infiltrated by Communists in the 1940's. (possibly stemming from SUBJECT's connection with Dr. Homer P. RAINEY)

The question is, how did Malcolm Wallace, a convicted murderer, tainted by a suspected Communist background, manage to achieve the security clearance levels necessary to work for defense contractors of that time period? A possible answer could possibly lie in the article Mark and I found in *The Dallas Morning news,* dated May 13, 1984:

In 1961, Wallace left Texas to go to Anaheim, Calif., to work for Ling Electronics. The change of jobs is what prompted the 1961 background check, said one of the former Navy intelligence officers. The officer, who conducted the background check, said "There was an investigation; that I can verify." He asked that his name not be used. The second Navy intelligence officer, who supervised the Texas end of the background check and now works in Dallas, confirmed that the report was compiled and forwarded to Washington.

Wallace had been active in politics while at the University of Texas, and authorities who investigated the Kinser murder said they found information linking Wallace to Communist Party activity in the United States, according to one investigator, who also wished that his name not be used.

Former Texas Ranger Clint Peoples, who investigated the Kinser murder, said the Navy intelligence officer who compiled the background report indicated to him in November 1961 that Johnson may have been a factor behind Wallace's employment with the defense contractors. "I was furious that they would even consider a security clearance for Wallace with the background he had," said Peoples, who is a U. S. Marshall in Dallas. "I asked him (the intelligence officer) how in the world Wallace could get the security clearance and he said 'politics,'" Peoples said. "I asked who could be so strong and powerful in politics that he could get a clearance for a man like this, and he said 'the vice president.'"

We now realized what Madeleine meant when she referred to Mac Wallace as "Lyndon's boy."

Chapter 15
"It's not what you know..."

What was emerging from our investigation was yet another reason why Wallace was so intensely loyal to Lyndon Johnson. He was being well taken care of by his benefactor, he being provided not only with protection, but a plausible cover. The vast network of the Texas based LTV companies would be an ideal home for Malcolm Wallace, a place where he would continually be on call.

In 1952, Temco (where Wallace first started his career with defense contractors following his murder conviction) was a fairly new company. Robert McCulloch founded the company shortly after World War II with the financial backing of oil millionaire, D. Harold Byrd and others. It was considered a risky venture - trying to make money in a military aircraft business without a war. McCulloch struggled for years to make the venture profitable, and by 1959 was showing annual sales in excess of 100 million dollars. In that year, D. Harold Byrd approached James Ling, the founder of Ling-Altec and suggested that the two companies would fare much better as a merged team, Ling-Altec supplying the expertise in electronics while Temco operated the airframe manufacturing end of the business. Together they would form a viable prime systems contractor. The merger was successful and in 1959 Temco was brought into Ling's company under the new name of Temco Electronics & Missiles Company. But Ling and Byrd were not finished.

The opportunity to take over a heavyweight company - the Chance Vought Corporation, presented itself. Chance Vought was a "real" working aircraft production company. The World War II "Corsair" gull-wing navy fighter was one of its more famous productions. The details of this acquisition are detailed in the book- **LING. THE RISE, FALL AND RETURN OF A TEXAS TITAN. (by Stanley H. Brown, 1972- Atheneum)**

"....a couple of weeks later, Ling announced - as he legally was required to do- that he and Ling-Temco owned more than 10 per cent of Chance Vought. He asked its management for a meeting. Two encounters took place in mid-January. ....Chance Vought struck back with a civil antitrust suit against Ling-Temco. It would later be reinforced by the announcement of a proposed antitrust action by the Department of Justice. Some people have suggested that the government's action was brought simply as the result of Chance Vought entreaties to Washington. Ling blamed it on Attorney General Robert F. Kennedy and from then on considered him his enemy.... ....There was a strong feeling in Texas in those days, supported by Texans in Washington, that the Kennedys' were systematically attempting to wreak as much havoc as they could among the backers of Lyndon Johnson. Ling's support of Johnson against John Kennedy in 1960 apparently put him in that category." (end quote)

Eventually the suit was settled in Ling's favor, and the merger of Vought Corporation brought into existence the defense powerhouse known since as LTV - Ling Temco Vought.

Ling, like other businessmen, measured his company's success by its relative position on the "Fortune 500" list - a yearly list of the nation's most prosperous companies. In 1959, with annual sales of around 48 million dollars, Ling-Altec didn't even appear on the prestigious list.

But after the acquisition of Temco and quickly thereafter, Chance Vought, the name not only appeared, but leaped steadily upward. By the end of 1960, LTV occupied place number 285 on the Fortune 500, with annual sales of about 148 million dollars. In 1962 the company reached number 158. In 1965 sales hit a new high of 336 million. In 1967 with sales over 1.5 billion, LTV would vault to position number 38.

A large part of the profitableness of LTV for many years was attributable to their being awarded (in February of 1964) the contract for the Navy A-7 light-attack aircraft, used in the Vietnam war. Over 450 units of another version, the A-7D, were sold to the Air Force.

LTV was not the only Texas-based company to benefit financially from the Vietnam conflict. General Dynamics, of Fort Worth, Texas produced the F-111 fighter aircraft.

The Texas based Brown and Root company, (major supporters of Lyndon Johnson throughout his political career) secured the multi-billion dollar contract to develop Camh Ranh Bay into a deep-water port in Vietnam. Bell Helicopter, of Fort Worth, Texas, supplied the majority of the thousands of helicopters used in the war.

The contract to build an extensive radio communications network connecting South Vietnam, Laos, and Thailand was awarded to the International Division of Collins Radio, a Dallas-based company.

Craig Roberts, author of *"Kill Zone, A Sniper Looks at Dealey Plaza"* (Consolidated Press International, Tulsa, Ok.) writes an interesting chapter concerning some of these companies, and others:

"Late in the war in Vietnam, information circulated among the fighting forces that one major stockholder of Bell

172

Helicopter just happened to be a "trust" whose beneficiary was Lady Bird Johnson. This same entity also was rumored to be a major stockholder in General Dynamics of Fort Worth, the Builder of the F-111."

Roberts set out to confirm or deny these rumors by inquiring of the Securities & Exchange Commission (SEC) as to the investors of these companies. He writes:

"My direct question on the fax was: "Who owned the controlling interest, or was a major stockholder, in the following U.S. corporations between 1960-68: Bell Helicopter, General Dynamics, Colt Firearms, Ford Motor Company, Boeing-Vertol, McDonnell Aircraft, and Douglas Aircraft?" One week Later I received a telephone call from a female assistant to the addressee. In a somewhat mystified sounding voice, she said that she had spent the day looking for the records of the above corporations concerning the dates in question, but had failed to locate them. She said this was most unusual-that those particular records were missing. She went on to say that it was possible, due to the passage of time, that the records may have been transferred to the National Archives. Maybe I should try there. But before I could write the National Archives, my original letter evidently surfaced at the SEC. On July 29th, 1992, I received a letter with the following statements: This is to acknowledge your letter concerning the above referenced. We are unable to provide the information you are in need of because the files have been disposed of in accordance with the Commission's Records Control Schedule (17 CFR 200.80f...") In a country that archives over 200 years of paperwork, including such important items as World War I memorandums on the procurement procedures for pack mules, World War II technical manuals on obsolete equipment, and records of telephone calls made from various obscure offices during the FDR years, I found it incredible that records dealing with some of the country's corporate giants had been

"disposed of." I was disappointed. Another door had been slammed shut by the bureaucracy."

Roberts, along with a host of other writers, investigators and researchers point out that none of this profit making could have taken place without a war, and the direction that President Kennedy was headed was not for a protracted engagement into Vietnam. Instead, he wanted to pull the existing military advisors and personnel out of the country, stating that it was ultimately a South Vietnamese conflict that must be fought by South Vietnamese.

On October 31, 1963 in a press conference, Kennedy publicly announced his intention to withdraw a thousand men from South Vietnam by the end of 1963. A reporter asked him about troop reductions in the far east. Here is the entire question and Kennedy's response:

"[REPORTER:] Mr. President, back to the question of troop reductions, are any intended in the far east at the present time - particularly in Korea and is there any speedup in the withdrawal from Vietnam intended?

[PRESIDENT KENNEDY:] Well as you know, when Secretary McNamara and General Taylor came back, they announced that we would expect to withdraw a thousand men from South Vietnam before the end of the year. And there has been some reference to that by General Harkins. If we're able to do that, that will be our schedule. I think the first unit, the first contingent, would be 250 men who are not involved in what might be called front-line operations. It would be our hope to lessen the number of Americans there by a thousand as the training intensifies and is carried on in South Vietnam."

Twenty two days later, Kennedy was killed. Lyndon Johnson, two days after the assassination, launched upon a course that would commit hundreds of thousands of troops to the conflict in South Vietnam. The war would last a decade, and cost over 58,000 American lives.

But certain American business interests would reap a fortune, and certain Texas Business interests, thanks to LBJ, would fare even better. As Robert Sherrill notes in his book, *"The Accidental President"* (Pyramid 1968):

"The Pentagon spends more money than the annual net income from all the corporations in America; half of its procurement money goes to 25 companies. Whether out of weakness or collusion, Johnson has permitted these war industrialists to have a free rein with his administration. But it is a fair exchange; the war contractors use him, and he uses the war contracts to tighten his political hold at home in Texas and throughout the nation. Thus we find Texas in 1967 moving into second place, displacing New York behind California, in war profiteering. Thus we also find the White House directing Lockheed-Georgia Co. to establish sub-assembly plants for the world's largest military airplane in the home districts of three key House committee chairmen (see Don Oberdorfer, Chicago Daily News Service, Feb. 18, 1967).

The bounty of the Johnson war machine is so great that it pours upon the ground and rusts and rots. The General Accounting Office discovered that so much un-needed equipment and supplies had been sent to Vietnam at one point that $32.9 million of it was just lying around.

It was a banner year for chemical companies, with napalm output alone reaching 50,000,000 pounds a month. The GAO discovered Mathieson Chemical Corporation making 65 percent profits on missile fuel. With the space program in a momentary lull, the electronics companies needed work, so Johnson capitulated to the generals and agreed (over McNamara's protests) to build a $5 billion

175

anti-missle system aimed at China (to be expanded to the $40 billion anti-Russian version later). And in addition to their really big war work, the steel companies were tossed little lagniappes, such as $5 million contracts to produce 50,000 miles of barbed wire and 5 million steel fence posts to build the McNamara Line between North and South Vietnam.

The picture was so clear that even some Senators could see it for what it was - "blood money profits... the profits of bloodletting," in the words of Wayne Morse."
(End quote)

It was Johnson's reciprocal relationship with Texas business interests that made it possible for Wallace, a cold-blooded murderer, to hold employment in an industry that provided a perfect cover. A closer look at one of these LBJ associates becomes an important next step.

Chapter 16
A Closer Look at the Colonel

Knowing when and where to invest for war was the key. Look at the beginning of the LTV empire for example. One of its early large investors, the previously mentioned D. Harold Byrd, was previously a stockholder in Temco Corporation, a company that was trying to make money in an aircraft business, but without the benefit of a war. It was Byrd's suggestion to Ling that they should consider merging the two entities into a viable defense oriented company. As pointed out in the previous chapter, LTV went on to grow, gather strength and breadth, and prosper, largely due to military contracts and the war in Vietnam.

The aircraft procurement program of the United States committed over six billion dollars for the purchase of military aircraft during the fiscal year of 1963-1964 alone. LTV's award of the A-7 was one of the largest.

A few weeks before the November, 1963 assassination, Byrd and partner James Ling, both prominent supporters of Johnson, bought over 130,000 shares of LTV stock . A month earlier, in October of 1963, Ling and another investor, Troy Post, another supporter and friend of LBJ, bought additional shares of LTV stock. The price of LTV stock varied in a range of $13 to $19 a share in 1963, but by 1967 this same stock grew to a value of $203; truly an outstandingly astute investment, especially in a market (1963) where aerospace investments had been in a decline, as compared to the stock market in general.

When we began to look a little closer at D. Harold Byrd (nephew of the famous Admiral Byrd), there was one major detail that jumped out at us. It wasn't the fact that he was a staunch right-winger and a personal friend of Lyndon Johnson. Nor was it the fact that he founded the Civil Air Patrol. (An organization to which Lee Harvey Oswald once belonged) What intrigued us was the fact that D. Harold Byrd, Dallas millionaire and oil tycoon, was the owner of the Texas School Book Depository Building. It was from this building's sixth floor, that a fusillade of shots ended the life of President Kennedy.

The startling discovery of D. Harold Byrd's ownership of the Book Depository building came from an article written by researcher William Weston, and appeared in the September, 1993 issue of Third Decade. I contacted Mr. Weston and talked at length with him about his research into "that monolith of enigma...the Texas School Book Depository Building."

Indeed, Weston assured me, Colonel Byrd purchased the building at 411 Elm Street in 1936, to manufacture air conditioning equipment. Later the building was leased out to various tenants, such as the John Sexton Company, a wholesale restaurant and grocery supply company. Apparently the Sexton Company vacated the premises sometime in 1962.

A few months before the assassination, the School Book Depository Company became the new tenants, moving from their former location across the street - the Dal-Tex building. That fact alone should have made investigators suspicious. The tenants of the Elm Street building - used as the platform for the assassination - had just recently moved in! To back up that fact, an FBI report, dated November 23, 1963 is quoted in Weston's article:

"Roy S. Truly, Warehouse Manager, Texas School Book Depository, advised that the Texas School Book Depository has occupied the building at 411 Elm street for only a few months. Prior to this time, the building was occupied by a wholesale grocery company engaged in supplying restaurants and institutions and during the course of their occupancy, the floors of the building became oil soaked and this oil was found to be damaging the stock of the School Book Depository theron. In view of this, they had instituted a process of covering the floor with sheets of plywood. The process was being performed by the regular warehouse employees whenever they had slack periods of work."

Actually, Harold Norman, in his interview with me discredited the last part of the above FBI statement. Norman, you recall stated that there was an outside contractor that was employed to repair the flooring, and that building workers were used in assisting the crew.

Weston seems to think that the timing of the move-in was no accident. He states in his article:

"Not much is known about this company (Bear in mind there is a distinction between the TSBD as a company, and the TSBD building, which was at 411 Elm Street.) or the people who worked for it, yet from the little information that can be gathered, I believe the direction of the evidence points only one way: that the organizers of the plot had complete control of the Book Depository building."

Who arranged for this sudden transfer of tenants? Weston writes:

The man who brought about this transaction was a very successful oil tycoon named D. H. Byrd. He held the same ultraconservative political views as other Texas oil men, such as H. L. Hunt and Clint Murchison. Byrd was the founder of the Civil Air Patrol which he organized to help with coastal patrol during WWII. In 1943 he was given the rank of Colonel....If the move-in period was the summer of 1963, as the above FBI memo, based on Roy Truly's statement seems to indicate, then it would parallel other strange developments occurring at that time.

1. Lee Harvey Oswald was in New Orleans, busily trying to convince the world that he was pro-Castro. He was printing and publicly handing out leaflets, debating on radio, and being arrested in a street scuffle. All of this occurring in a relatively short period of time.

2. Plans were being formulated for a presidential visit to Texas. Later, Oswald would move back to Dallas, where Ruth Paine, a friend of his wife, would recommend that he apply for a job at the School Book Depository. He was hired immediately. "

Weston's research has revealed that the depository building was largely made up of office space, with the upper floors (fifth and sixth) being used as warehouse space. Of the 40 or so employees in the building, only 15 warehouse workers were allowed to use the stairway that accessed the upper floors. Anyone else was instructed to use the side by side freight elevators located near the stairway, on the north side of the building, or the passenger elevator that extended only to the fourth floor. This arrangement definitely kept upper-floor traffic to a minimum. If, as Weston suggests, the conspirators had complete control of the School Book Depository, this would help explain how the rifles, as well as the assassins got in and out of the building without detection. It also explains why Oswald, who quite possibly served as the assassination team's scapegoat, was so quickly zeroed in on as a suspect. Within minutes, building management determined that Oswald alone was missing and quickly provided the police at the scene with his address, along with his physical description.

Another thing that Weston pointed out was the appearance of the School Book Depository's written records that were turned over to the FBI and the Warren Commission. There were only three documents, as compared to the dozens of documents turned over by other employers of Oswald, and all three of these documents looked homemade and amateurish. Weston writes:

"The problematical features of the TSBD documents indicate that none of them are genuine. Either the real ones do not exist or they contain information that the company did not wish to make public. Such a casual attitude, if not outright disdain, for the simplest forms of documentation leads to an increase in our curiosity about the kind of people who worked for this company."

The actions of the School Book Depository occupants, though suspicious, seem to pale in contrast to the actions of it's owner, Mr. Byrd. Within weeks following the assassination, he commissioned his own carpentry crew to remove the "Oswald window" from the southeast corner of the sixth floor, replacing it with a look-alike. He then had built a custom showcase for it and prominently displayed the macabre death window at his home, among the dozens of animal trophies and souvenirs from around the world. After Col. Byrd's death, his son returned the window display to the Sixth Floor Museum in Dallas.

It is no wonder then, that a shroud of suspicion hangs over the rich and powerful Texans who befriended and supported Lyndon Johnson. During the research and investigation phase of this book I had opportunity to communicate with a retired member of the intelligence community, who told me about an event that he attended, a luncheon at the Petroleum Club in San Antonio, in 1973:

"I couldn't pass up the chance to ask Texas oil guys their view of the Hunt family being involved in JFK's death. After much laughter my host said, 'Hell, half of Dallas was in on it!'"

From what we have learned, Mark and I concur with that simple statement.

1973 Photo of **D.H. Byrd** (left, with white hat and dark coat) and **LBJ** at a UT football game. Friends for many years, Byrd was a political and financial supporter of Johnson, and the owner of the Texas School Book Depository building in Dallas.

Chapter 17
The Man in the Horn-Rimmed Glasses

Mark and I found ourselves so busy in the investigation that at one point we almost forgot about Loy.

Our thrust was mainly toward identifying Loy's superiors. Besides, Loy and Mary had no phone, and we were limited to communication by mail. We were sure that Loy would be excited by what we were discovering, but before we had a chance to tell him about the direction our research was taking, I received a note with a simple message from Loy:

"Dear Mark Collom & Glen Sample,

I am writing to ask for cancellation of procedure of the writing of this book.

At the present, have problems needing attention. Thanks anyway for your good efforts on this work.

Sincerely, Loy Factor

"What do we do now?" I asked Mark. I had immediately telephoned him with the bad news. Just as before, while at the hospital, when he had refused to resume his conversation with Mark and Larry, fear had again silenced Loy Factor. We were not going to be dissuaded in our research, however, as the scope of our investigation had grown much larger than Loy Factor. We had discovered someone far more important - we had found Malcolm Wallace.

"Let's try what we did before - let's write him a letter and try to convince him that he needs to continue to cooperate," was Mark's suggestion. I agreed that it was worth a try, and so I composed a letter, urging Loy to continue doing what he promised us he would do - telling the truth. I enumerated the many things that we had found verifying his story. I told him that the world deserved to hear the truth that only he has been willing to tell. I commended him for his bravery thus far in helping us find the real killers of President Kennedy, but at the same time told him that we would not, and could not stop what we had begun. I sent the letter, hoping for a favorable reply from Loy.

We wanted, if nothing else, to show him photographs of Malcolm Wallace, but not by mail. We wanted to see the expression on Loy's face. What we needed, at the very least, was one more visit with Loy.

In the meantime, there was work to be done. One task that I was particularly interested in was trying to find personal friends and fellow workers of Wallace.

Ling Electronics, the company that Wallace worked for from 1961 until 1969, was located in Southern California, just a few miles from my home. I phoned the personnel department and asked if there was anyone in the company that would remember Mr. Wallace, even though it had been over 25 years since his employment. I was referred to a long-time employee, Joe Bloomberg, who had actually worked under Wallace for many years. I didn't tell Joe that I was working on a book about the Kennedy assassination, a subject that tends to close more doors than it opens. Instead, I told him (and truthfully so) that I was researching a book that deals with crimes that have been committed to protect government officials. I explained that Malcolm Wallace was simply one of the characters in our book, and asked him if he could shed some light on the man that he had worked side-by-side with for nearly nine years. He graciously agreed.

My interview with Joe Bloomberg took place at Ling Electronics, in Anaheim, California. He gave me a tour of the facility, which manufactures devices that vibrate various types of electronic circuitry, simulating the harsh conditions that these components would encounter in missiles or jet aircraft.

I wanted to know what kind of person Wallace was. How did others view him? Joe was able to verify that Wallace appeared to have a problem with alcohol. He explained that the company had put up with Wallace's drinking for a long time. He described a serious automobile accident on a nearby freeway that nearly cost him his life. "But I always liked him. Everyone did. He was very intelligent, and performed his job quite well."

Then I asked about his security clearance. "That was one thing that was kind of strange," Bloomberg recalled. "You see, we worked in the contracts department and Mac was my boss, but he didn't have the clearance necessary to read some of the paperwork, so I would have to do it."

Odd indeed, I thought, for a company to hire a convicted murderer, (which a few in the company were well aware of) who was also an alcoholic, and had been recently stripped of the security clearance necessary for him to properly perform his job.

Something else I learned about Wallace was consistent in the observations of everyone who knew him: No one knew him. Not one person could describe his wife, or even name her. No one knew how many children he had. He never talked about himself, his life, his politics, and never mentioned his relationship with Lyndon Johnson. Hence, when it was later learned (after he had left the company in 1969) that Wallace had been convicted of murder, and was connected with Lyndon Johnson, no one could believe it. Malcolm Wallace was an enigma.

I asked about his absences from work. Other than absences that were ostensibly from his heavy drinking, Wallace occasionally traveled to Texas, where his family resided, and where the parent company headquarters were located.   He was sent on other projects as well - the construction of a particle beam accelerator at Stanford University, for example. A strange project to be involved in for someone without a security clearance.

Joe had, at my request, looked through his assortment of old company photographs, thinking that he surely had a good photo or two of Wallace. But strangely, all he was able to find was a single photograph, showing Wallace standing far off in the distance. Only two things could be learned from the photograph. He had gained a little weight (compared with our photographs of a younger Wallace) and he was wearing horn-rimmed glasses. The photograph was taken sometime around 1963.

This seemingly insignificant fact might not register with someone who has never studied the Kennedy assassination, but I instantly recognized it as another small piece of evidence linking Wallace to the assassination. Why? A Dealey Plaza witness to the assassination, Richard R. Carr, reported to police and officials that he had seen a heavyset man in a tan jacket, and wearing horn-rimmed glasses, standing in one of the sixth floor windows of the School Book Depository Building, a minute or so before the assassination. A few minutes later, Carr said, the same man was seen hurriedly walking away from the building. Carolyn Walthers also saw what she describes as a brown-coated man, standing next to another man with a rifle. She was not certain which of the upper-floors of the depository she observed them on. James Worrell Jr. said he saw a man in a suit coat exit swiftly out the rear door of the depository shortly after the shooting. He did not get a look at the man's face, but his sighting matches that of Bill Shelly, a depository worker, who also spotted a brown-coated man run out the back door of the book depository.

All of our earlier photographs of Wallace, taken in his university days, show him wearing wire-framed glasses. But the Ling photograph clearly shows that Wallace had changed the style of his glasses.

Going back to the 1961 murder of Henry Marshall, a composite drawing was made of the man seen by gas station operator Nolan Griffin. Griffin described to investigators a man wearing horn-rimmed glasses, who stopped at his station a couple of days before Marshall was found dead, asking for directions to the Marshall place. This drawing was at first thought to be the likeness of Billie Sol Estes, who later implicated "Mac" Wallace as the murderer.

At one critical point in our conversation, I broached the Kennedy assassination with Joe Bloomberg, asking, if he remembered the reactions of his staff on that day. Joe described the shock that spread through the office, how the secretaries were crying and so on. "We shut the whole place down and everyone went home," Joe said. Then I asked if he remembered Malcolm Wallace's reaction to the shooting of the president, since Wallace worked in the same office as

Bloomberg did. "I don't recall Mac being there that day," was Joe's casual reply.

But Joe was not the only person close to Malcolm Wallace who did not know his whereabouts on November 22. Neither did his wife.

I must credit the late Austin researcher Jay Harrison for helping me find the former Virginia Ledgerwood, ex-wife of Malcolm Wallace, not more that 15 miles from my home in Southern California. I had tried many times to get an interview with Virginia. (now remarried). When I finally got a terse phone call from her one evening, I sensed that she was not terribly pleased to discuss the subject of Wallace, and was generally interested in getting it over with, so I would stop writing her.

She explained that the two of them were married in 1963, a hasty arrangement, motivated by an unplanned pregnancy. On the day of the Kennedy assassination, she vividly remembers that she and Malcolm (Mac) had already separated and she was at the home of her mother, with their newborn daughter. She had no contact with him, and does not know of where Mac was on that fateful day of the assassination.

She did tell me that Malcolm once discussed with her his friendship with Mr. and Mrs. Lyndon Johnson, although most of his former history remained a mystery to her. Malcolm was, to say the least, a quiet man.

Chapter 18
Farewell Loy Factor

Hello Glen & Mark;

Thinking about you and wondering if   you are continuing with the book.

I'm in Willow Haven Nursing Home in Tonkawa. Would like to hear from you.

Loy Factor.

The note was dated January 31, 1994. It had been a few months since we had heard from Loy. He had not responded to my letter urging him to continue to help us, and now he seemed to be giving us an indication of his change of heart. I quickly looked up the phone number of the Willow Haven Nursing Home, and within a few minutes was talking to Loy.

Loy sounded tired and weak. He said that he had undergone another surgery, removing the rest of his remaining foot. Having been plagued with a serious infection, he had come close to dying. He wanted to know how the book was coming; I told him that we were still working on it and that we were planning another trip in a few weeks. He said that he would like to see us. I took this to mean that he would like to help us further and told him that we would call him when we had finalized our travel plans.

We arranged for this, our third, interview with Loy, to take place on March 19, 1994 at the nursing home in Tonkawa. Mark and I decided that for this interview we would use a video camera so as to record his reaction to the Wallace photographs.

Loy was waiting for us in his wheelchair, just inside the lobby of the nursing home. I couldn't help feeling that even though he was both ill and disabled, and certainly belonged in this place, he looked so out of place. Loy Factor, who once rode Brahma bulls in the rodeos, who hunted, fished and lived life in a rough and rugged way, was now sitting in an old folks home with a comforter spread across his lap.

The nursing staff was helpful in arranging for us to use a quiet office for our meeting with Loy. He agreed to the use of the video camera, although we could tell he looked quite uncomfortable in front of it.

Our strategy had been planned on the drive up from Tulsa. We would not bring up the subject of the conspirators or the assassination until later. Instead, we would engage Loy in a discussion concerning the details about his release from prison. Then I would hand Loy a handful of photographs and ask him if he would take a look at them. We didn't want to appear to attach too much importance to them.

Loy reached for the photographs and began studying them, slowly, one by one. After a full forty seconds, Mark broke the silence -

"Do you know who that is Loy?"

"Yeah..."

"Who is it?"

"It's Wallace."

"You're sure?"

"I'm sure."

"This is the man that you first met at the funeral of Sam Rayburn," I stated.

"That's him."

"The same man who later hired you to assist in President Kennedy's assassination."

"That's right."

Loy's face expressed volumes. There was no doubt in our minds at all - he recognized the photographs as the man known to him only as "Wallace". We then proceeded to tell Loy what we had come to learn about Wallace; his friendship and loyalty to Lyndon Johnson, his 1952 murder conviction. We asked him if there had ever been a hint that Wallace was working for Johnson. Loy said that the name of Johnson had never come up. In fact, he registered honest surprise when he learned of Wallace's link with Lyndon Johnson.

We read the notes from our interview with Harold Norman, which verified the presence of a table saw on the sixth floor. He listened with interest as we related our conversations with Madeleine Brown. He verified that Wallace did wear glasses, but was unable to recall what style, or anything else about his appearance on that fateful day.

"Loy, we still have a problem that we were hoping you could help us with," Mark said, looking Loy in the eye.

"We know that Malcolm Wallace, Lee Oswald and you were on the sixth floor of that building." Loy nodded.

"There's no doubt that you were there, and you've told us the truth about everything that you saw and heard."

"That's right," Loy responded.

"And we also know that you were paid money."

"That's right."

"But what we don't understand," I interjected, "is what were you paid for, if you didn't pull the trigger."

Loy looked at both of us. This question had come up before.

"Let me tell you what we think happened," I said, "and you tell us if we're right."

Loy nodded with approval. I had nothing to lose. Maybe a different approach to the question would be helpful.

"We think that you shot at the president, but purposefully missed, or you pretended to shoot your weapon and in the confusion the others assumed that you fired."

"I never fired a shot,' Loy responded. "They wanted me to shoot, but I didn't."

"Did you have a rifle in your hands?"

For the first, last, and only time, Loy answered that question in the affirmative.

"Yeah, they had a rifle for me, and I could have shot him, like they wanted me to, but   I didn't. I ejected a shell from the rifle, but it was never fired."

And so that's where Mark and I left it. Loy has been insistent, from his first revelation of his involvement, that he never pulled the trigger. He had confessed to a degree of involvement, even to the extent of aiming one of the weapons at the presidential motorcade and then escaping from the scene with the murderers and accepting money from them.   We had been told as much as Loy Factor was ever going to tell us.

"What about your family, Loy? What do you think their reaction will be to what you have revealed in our book?"

"Well," Loy said thoughtfully, "I just want people to know the truth."

"And what you've told us has been the truth, hasn't it Loy?"

"Yes, it's been the truth."

Less than seven weeks later, on May 5, 1994, Loy Factor passed away.

Chapter 19
"The Guilty Men"

In November of 2003, the History Channel ran a series of special programs during the 40th anniversary of the JFK assassination. The eleven hours of assassination programming included 3 new segments OF Nigel Turner's series "The Men Who Killed Kennedy"

"The Smoking Guns" was the first to air, taking to task the Secret Service and their possible complicity in the assassination. The medical evidence was discussed, followed by the story of mortician John Liggett, who was said to have had a part in reconstructing Kennedy's wounds.

Next aired "The Love Affair", in which a woman named Judyth Baker claimed she had been Lee Harvey Oswald's mistress. Together they worked on an anti-Castro murder plot along with David Ferrie and Guy Banister. The claim was also made that Oswald was trying to stop the assassination plot against JFK.

But the third segment - "The Guilty Men." was no doubt the most provocative. Who were the Guilty Men? The identity of one of them was announced during the first 30 seconds of the program.

Barr McClellan, author of *Blood, Money & Power: How LBJ Killed JFK,* sat before the camera and stated with certain confidence:

"I know, as attorney for Lyndon Johnson, that he murdered John Kennedy. He murdered John Kennedy to become president and to avoid prison and there is no doubt in my mind."

Then followed the steady building of McClellan's case, with interviews, photographs, first person accounts, fingerprint identification, all pointing to LBJ as the mastermind in the Kennedy assassination.

I too was interviewed by Turner, who incorporated much of our research of Malcolm Wallace and the murder of Doug Kinser in the film. I contributed the newspaper clippings from my extensive research collection, and also told of the account that Kinser's own daughter reported to me, that LBJ closely monitored the 10 day trial of Wallace, sending runners from his hotel to the courthouse to keep him informed.

The *Guilty Men* segment captured American's attention like no previous JFK program ever had. DVD sales of the History Channel's presentation soared. Angry phone calls to the LBJ library by some viewers of the *Guilty Men* expressed outrage, and some even threatened to tear the library down. Lady Bird Johnson, who in 1984, refused to comment on Billie Sol Estes' claims that her husband had ordered the death of Henry Marshall and others, joined several LBJ associates in writing to the History Channel. Jack Valenti, Bill Moyers, Jimmy Carter and Gerald R. Ford all rallied to stop the further televising of what they called "very bad journalism, the worst they had ever seen." They demanded that a rebuttal be presented to counter the error of the *Guilty Men* allegations. All DVD sales of the *GM* documentary and the other two segments (unrelated to the LBJ accusations) were halted. Agreement was made to NEVER air the programs again. Existing *GM* DVDs became collector's items and many were bootlegged and sold online. At the present time the documentaries are available on YouTube but nowhere else.

The response from the public was predictable. What was there to hide? Why the censorship? The LBJ camp had successfully strong-armed the History Channel into dropping one of their most successful programs, producing a rebuttal program, and offering an apology to Lady Bird Johnson.

04-02-2004
Dateline: NEW YORK
In response to an uproar caused by a History Channel documentary that claimed President Lyndon Johnson was involved in the Kennedy assassination, the network will air a challenge to that program by a panel of three historians.

The special, airing 8 p.m. EDT Wednesday, is called "The Guilty Men: An Historical Review."

The one-hour program is meant to rebut last November's broadcast of "The Guilty Men," which was based in part on a book published in 2003 by Barr McClellan, who claims the law firm he quit a quarter-century ago was involved in convoluted plots that link Johnson to at least 11 deaths, including President Kennedy...

The historians chosen to examine the allegations were author Robert Dallek, an authority on LBJ's career; Stanley Kutler, a law professor at the University of Wisconsin and Thomas Sugrue, an author and teacher at the University of Pennsylvania.

On Wednesday, April 7th, 2003 the program aired. Although the historians concluded that the documentary was *"entirely unfounded and does not hold up to scrutiny,"* there was very little scrutiny to be found in this special review. No mention was made of the damning evidence in the murder of Doug Kinser. Nothing concerning the Texas grand jury findings linking LBJ to the murder of Henry Marshall was even mentioned, let alone "scrutinized." What of the four letters of communication between the Justice Department and Billie Sol Estes? These were all key elements of the *Guilty Men* documentary. Where was the scrutiny there? And where was their scrutiny of the fingerprint evidence as presented by Nathan Darby? What was the panel's explaination of why Polk Shelton and John Cofer, both known as LBJ lawyers, represented Malcolm Wallace in his murder trial? What was their explanation of the threats to the jury during the 10 day trial? And why, according to the three historians was Malcolm Wallace's sentence suspended, allowing him to walk away a free man and soon after secure employment in a company that was co-founded and run by D. Harold Byrd, a close friend and political supporter of LBJ, and owner of the Texas School Book Depository Building? The Historians ignored the above details, yet had the nerve to call the program *"An Historical Review"*

Immediately the responses posted on the History Channel's website reflected a broad based disappointment in the program. One viewer wrote:

The American public has been denied the truth once again. The evidence is out there, and The Guilty Men only scratched the surface. Mac Wallace was a murderer, Estes and Baker were extortionists, and LBJ was their leader. Estes has provided documented proof that LBJ ordered the murder of Henry Marshall and others, and has provided a list of killings, which included JFK, LBJ was responsible for. The LBJ group doesn't want this coming to national attention, and once again the media submitted to being a part of the coverup.

Another viewer wrote:

Tonight's rebuttal panel program to The Guilty Men documentary was amateurish at best. Robert Dallek said there is no censorship in America. He said this on the very channel that censored "The Guilty Men." Stanley Kutler said the Warren Commission was published in 1965. He said it twice. Shouldn't a historian know it was published in

1964??   If the HC censors any program from further view, it should be this one.

Oddly, Barr McClellan was never contacted, nor were any of the people involved in the film interviewed. Not one phone call to Nathan Darby, Nigel Turner, or myself. McClellan was quick to respond to the action of the History Channel in censoring "*The Guilty Men*". He stated in a press release:

"....That was a mistake. The public deserves to see "The Guilty Men," and judge for itself. Not only should the History Channel re-broadcast "The Guilty Men," as it does so many other programs, but it should also allot time for a reply to the panel's evaluation to be presented.

This historical dispute should be judged not by historians, but by the public, after hearing historical evidence -- just as a criminal trial is resolved not by judges, but by a jury..."

And so this is where it ended. Since then Gerald Ford, Lady Bird Johnson, and Jack Valenti have all passed away. Perhaps other attempts at presenting the view that a strong Texas connection exists in the assassination of JFK will be more successful. Until then, *The Men on the Sixth Floor* and *Blood, Money and Power* continue to fill the void.

Chapter 20
The Mac Wallace Fingerprint

It was little more than a smudge. For that reason this particular fingerprint was determined to be unidentified, or perhaps unidentifiable and was filed away in the National Archives for over 35 years, along with hundreds of other Warren Commission exhibits, until its importance and identity was clarified in 1998.

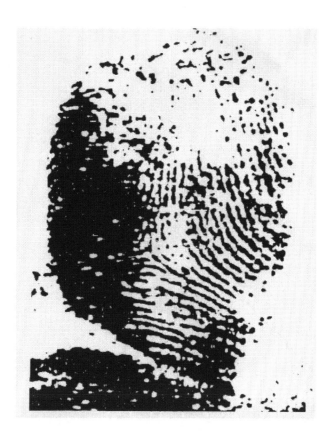

The print in question was found on "box A" – the designation given to the box of books that supposedly served as a "rifle rest" for Lee Harvey Oswald. But this particular print, (box A, print number 29), was not that of Oswald. Neither did it match the employees of the book depository or any of the police, FBI or Secret Service agents who swarmed over the building within minutes of the assassination.

The box in the dead center of this photo is "Box A" where the unidentified print #29 was found. The location of these boxes was the southeast corner of the sixth floor Texas School Book Depository in Dallas Texas.

How this fingerprint was discovered, analyzed and eventually matched with a 1951 fingerprint card of Malcolm Wallace is an interesting story – and the impelling force behind this match up was, of all people, an ex Dallas Cop.

The fingerprints that covered the boxes piled strategically in the "snipers nest" became the study for a man who made the Kennedy assassination his life's work. To say he was a researcher is a statement that is less than complete. Jay Harrison was, on November 22, 1963, a Dallas policeman, who, within 5 minutes of the shooting of the president was at the scene of the crime.

I met Jay online in 1996, sometime after *The Men on the Sixth Floor* was published. The book, rich in detail about Malcolm Everett Wallace, was the reason why Jay contacted me. He was obsessed with Mac Wallace and I guess I was too. He wrote:

> *I believe that you and I have more than one thing in common! Malcolm Everett Wallace, a man of may interests and vocations…and friends…among other attributes and faults, and ignored by most historians… and more importantly ignored by probable mis/dis-information sources. I buy very few conspiracy books until such time as I can acquire them in the $1 or $2 "special close-out" section at Half Price Books, here in Austin.*
>
> *Two authors recently released their works: Jim Hosty (a fictional writer) claiming a (inaccurate) space in the non-fiction/historical world, and "Assignment – Oswald" , Arcade Publishing 1996 ($25.95) NOTE: way overpriced for a "fictional account" of some of the events that took place in Oct. – Dec. '63. And two hitherto unknown guys from California named Sample & Collom who co-authored a yet-to-be recognized historic classic.*
>
> *Reading this book was quite an experience for me…. with the exception of the material on LOY FACTOR (a person then unknown to me) I had the strangest felling that somebody was accessing MY data base.*

I learned from my correspondence and phone conversations with Jay that his depth of research was phenomenal, and his history as a researcher was legend – but only to a few. He was very cautious about his work on the assassination, always working in the shadows, under the radar. He no doubt held the record for the number of years spent investigating the Kennedy murder and it was evident that he was proud of it. He wrote:

I was a reserve on the Dallas Police Department assigned to the Criminal Intelligence Section on the day of the assassination. I joined the department in early 1961 and left it in 1968. My DPD ID# was 858 and my badge was #125. I was the first reserve officer to receive the "Certificate of Merit" from the DPD (a very prestigious award) as a direct result of my research and undercover work on the "left and right" wings.

I was at the TSBD within 5 minutes of the event. I had the Black Muslim Church under surveillance during the motorcade. It was about ½ mile away from the TSBD.

Subsequently, I was on the guard team for Governor Connally and on Sunday morning I was in the basement of City Hall involved in the security for the transfer of Oswald to the County Sheriff's Dept.

I am identified in the Warren Commission Vol XII, pg. 356, line 16. This is in the testimony of Sgt. Donald Francis Steele who I was with ALL morning long at Dallas Police Headquarters on Sunday morning and just prior to (5 minutes) BEFORE the shooting of Oswald by Ruby. I drove the car out of the basement that preceded Lt. Rio Sam Pierce that gave the opportunity for Ruby to enter the driveway entrance when the "crowd" was split to allow our cars to exit. Ruby was still in the WU (Western Union) office at the time I left.

I personally have met and talked (at length) to George DeMohrenschildt, Bertha Cheek, George Lincoln Rockwell, Edwin Walker, the Paines, Jack Ruby....and

knew personally Nick McDonald, J.D Tippit, Jessie Currie,
Jack Revill, just to cite a few.

My military training and assignments in the US
Army, during the "Korean Conflict" was in intelligence and
communications. My primary MOS was 1766 (high speed
radio) operator (morse code) and I spent over a year in the
Joint Chiefs of Staff Communications Center in the
Pentagon.

After my "active duty" I spent 6 years in the reserves
(mandatory) and was assigned to a 6 man SIRA team.
(Strategic Intelligence Research and Analysis)

For over 42 years I have done genealogical research
on specific persons, their families, ancestors and
descendants. That experience has been critical to the
establishment of great depth of provable data on the
individuals and sub-events that I research in this endeavor.

Shortly before Jay's death in May of 2005 he asked
Walt Brown to box up his *one ton* of research and take it to
New Jersey for safekeeping. Brown's description of Jay
Harrison's research records is impressive:

...When people get the chance to view the materials
in the Jay Harrison Archive, which I someday hope to be
able to scan and put on cd's, they will realize that nobody
has ever equaled the meticulous research he did. Mary
Ferrell was lionized for having a data base that involved over
8,000 names. Jay's was over 26,000, and it includes masses
of "Vital Records" data--birth certificates, death
certificates--blue originals, not xerox copies--that simply
boggle the mind.

Hopefully the above gives the reader a clear
description of the high caliber researcher Jay was. Through
our communication, he was able to help me with several

areas of research, which were included in a later edition of our book. He clarified my mistaken notion that Malcolm Wallace was related to Henry Agard Wallace, former Vice President as well as former Secretary of Agriculture. His excellent genealogical research helped me find and interview Mac Wallace's ex-wife, Virginia Ledgerwood. I benefited greatly from his file on Wallace which was deep and rich.

Looking back on our communications, I see now a subtle hint about the Malcolm Wallace fingerprint. He wrote:

If we are both right (which we are), SOME knowledge can be potentially very dangerous. You were FIRST to put him there (in print). I am going to PROVE that he was there!

It was no doubt during this time that Jay was maneuvering for access to the arrest records of Wallace, including the fingerprint file. He never disclosed any more than the above about this "project" of his.

About the same time (1996) I was also corresponding with Stephen Pegues, a colorful native Texan who was busy writing a book he called "The Texas Mafia". Pegues was close to Billie Sol Estes; a long time friend of the family. Pegues, like Jay, was a great researcher, but also a proud Texas historian. I think it was Stephen who, more than anyone else helped me understand the thinking of a "True Texan."

Pegues, like Jay was an early reader of *The Men on the Sixth Floor*. And, like Jay, Pegues was very interested in Malcolm Wallace. Since it was Billie Sol Estes who first drew the connection between Wallace, LBJ, and the assassination of JFK, naturally Stephen Pegues was knowledgeable in this area and was attracted to the information in our book. It was in fact, Pegues who gave me the first of four "Estes documents" that we later included in a later edition of the book. His source for these important documents is yet another story.

Because of our common interests, I introduced Stephen Pegues to Jay Harrison. Before long, the two men struck up a friendship and combined their talents.

As the story goes, they were successful in setting up and interview with a family member of Malcolm Wallace. The interview was to be on the September 3, 1997. But that morning Jay was shocked to find that Stephen had died of a heart attack the night before, or early that morning. This was a terrible blow to the normally reclusive Jay Harrison. His reclusiveness transformed into paranoia. He called me the next day to tell me of Stephen's untimely death, shaken, his voice fearful. I remembered a package of notes and clippings that Stephen had just sent to me. I grabbed the envelope and looked at the date: August 28, 1997 – six days prior to his death. Included in the package was a reply from the Chicago Police Department concerning a Freedom of Information request for information on the death of former Estes business partner Coleman Wade. The letter informed Stephen that no information could be found. A similar letter from the FBI concerning information requested about the deaths of Ike Rogers, Harold Orr, Coleman Wade, Howard Pratt and Malcolm Everett Wallace. There was no record responsive to the FOIA request. The response was dated August 5, 1997.

The sudden death of Stephen Pegues haunted Jay until the day of his own death in 2005. After Jay's phone call, informing me of Stephen's death, our communication ended, but not Jay's determination. Undaunted, Jay Harrison hunted down the object of his obsession – the Mac Wallace fingerprint card. It came after years of legal wrangling with the Austin Police authorities.

During this period Jay started working with Barr McClellan, who was busy compiling research for his book,

Blood, Money and Power – How LBJ Killed JFK. McClellan's team of researchers, who included among others, Walt Brown, was instrumental in pushing the fingerprint project onward.

Meanwhile Mark and I got a tip that there was a group of Texas researchers who had matched a fingerprint found in the Texas School Book Depository with Wallace's fingerprint. Little else was known about this team but two names of its members – Barr McClellan and Jay Harrison. The information that we had was sparse, namely that the TSBD print was from "Box A" and could possibly be print number 20, 22, or 29 – or all three. The corresponding matching print was from a fingerprint card from Wallace's arrest record.

Our excitement was intensified and genuinely warranted. Mark and I were faced with the real possibility that Loy Factor's story would become more plausible, even more credible than ever before, based on real forensic evidence! I could not sleep for days. There had never been a doubt in my mind that the Factor story – leading to Mac Wallace – LBJ and the assassination of JFK was true. But now we would be able to prove it! We determined that we would launch an investigation of our own; not to preempt the Texas team, but to satisfy our own curiosity. We had no idea how or when, or even IF the other team was planning on releasing its information, and it seemed that it would be a simple task.

We needed to get Mac Wallace's fingerprint card. From what we knew, Wallace had been arrested in 1951 and fingerprinted by the Austin Police. My attempts to get the prints from them were fruitless. We learned that Mac had also been arrested in Dallas on public drunkenness charges in the early 60's. Our attempts to find these records were also disappointing. Attaining the latent fingerprint photos from the National Archives proved to be the easy part.

Finally we were able to come up with a poor quality copy of the 1951 Wallace print. Our next step was our most faulty. I found an organization called "S.C.A.F.O." – an acronym for Southern California Association of Fingerprint Officers. I emailed several of the members, explaining that I was a writer who was working on a story that involved examining some fingerprints. I invited anyone within the membership to contact me if they were interested in offering their professional opinions. Within a week, two or three did respond. I was most impressed by a young officer named Mike who specialized in fingerprint analysis in a nearby police department. He invited me to his office to show him what I had. His superior officer was also curious and joined the conversation. Their curiosity and my desire to have these prints compared influenced me to disclose the nature and source of the fingerprints. The Texas researchers, I later learned, had handled this in an entirely different way, by keeping the details of the prints secret, thereby allowing their expert to work "blind", without prejudice.

The initial examination of the prints convinced the fingerprint officers that they needed better prints. Going against official policy, they contacted Austin and requested the official fingerprint file of Malcolm Wallace, which they quickly obtained.

How disappointed we were to hear the words – "sorry, no match" come from our experts. Their explanation was that the prints were similar, with many matching points, there were too many dissimilar elements. The officers also indicated that their superiors advised them to drop the project and not connect the department to it in any fashion. We were not allowed to have possession of the requested official print, since it was the property of the department. Our fingerprint investigation came to a sad end.

Meanwhile the Texas group held a press conference on May 29, 1998. John Kelin was the first to report the details:

"A Texas-based assassination research group has identified a man believed to have left a previously unidentified fingerprint on a box making up the alleged "sniper's nest" on the sixth floor of the Texas School Book Depository, from which President Kennedy was allegedly assassinated in 1963.

Researcher Walt Brown, speaking on behalf of the Texas group, said at a May 29 press conference in Dallas that the fingerprints belong to Malcolm E. "Mac" Wallace, a convicted killer with ties to Lyndon Baines Johnson.

Brown presented data showing a 14-point match between Wallace's fingerprint card, obtained from the Texas Department of Public Safety, and the previously unidentified print, a copy of which was kept in the National Archives. The match was made by A. Nathan Darby, an expert with certification by the International Association of Identifiers.

According to members of the research group, this new evidence has been in the hands of the Dallas Police Department since May 12. The DPD passed it on to the Federal Bureau of Investigation.

Malcolm Wallace, convicted in a 1951 murder and suspected in others, was reportedly killed in an automobile accident in 1971. He has been linked to the death of Texas Agriculture Department investigator Henry Marshall, said to be close to uncovering felonious behavior by Billy Sol Estes and Lyndon Johnson.

The fact of Wallace's fingerprint in the so-called "sniper's nest" does not, of course, mean he pulled a trigger that day. Brown cited FBI fingerprint expert Sebastion Latona's testimony to the Warren Commission, in which Latona

209

stated that fingerprints can only be taken from a surface like cardboard within 24 hours of its origin.

Furthermore, "Wallace's print at the crime scene is hard evidence that corroborates the circumstantial evidence of Loy Factor's eyewitness account of Wallace's presence," said Texas researcher Richard Bartholomew. Loy Factor has claimed that he, Wallace, Lee Oswald, and a woman identified as "Ruth Ann" were present on the TSBD sixth floor as part of an assassination team.

According to Bartholomew, the same question was raised by the Dallas police on May 12. "The FBI's own textbook on fingerprint science teaches the basic concept of fingerprint evidence used in criminal investigation," he said. "Those who have an innocent reason to have handled the objects in question are eliminated from suspicion if their latent prints are present. Did Wallace have an innocent reason? No."

Mark and I posted our progress (or lack thereof) on our website, much to the chagrin of the Texas group and everyone else who looked to the fingerprint evidence to be the final word in the JFK conspiracy. Although I made an attempt to contact Nathan Darby to discuss our findings, I was unable to find him. I should have looked harder, because when I finally did meet Darby, years later, I was forced to look much harder at what our "experts" had determined.

I first saw and heard Nathan Darby as he appeared in his interview in "The Guilty Men" documentary. I was very impressed with his confidence in his fingerprint match. "It's a match!" he insisted. "There's no doubt about it – the finger that made the latent print and the finger that was on the fingerprint card is the SAME finger! If I was to die today, my final declaration would be: It's a MATCH!"

After watching Darby confidently defend his work I decided to again try to contact him. This time I was successful. Several phone conversations with this wonderful gentleman convinced me that we must meet in person. Nathan invited Mark and I to Austin, and we accepted. We spent the better part of a day with Mr. Darby at his home in Austin. There he explained, as would a schoolteacher, the various aspects of fingerprint analysis to us. He related step by step how he was presented with the prints, how he was never told to what case the fingerprints were related. He was paid as a professional for a professional comparison. Later he gave us notes and details of a third analysis of the print evidence. Since I am not an expert, I have no way of confirming Darby's print results, but what I can say is that his explanation of the evidence, his confidence in his results and his sterling character, along with my personal examination of the prints, lead me to the conclusion that the match is correct. But you be the judge. Look at the material that follows. Some of it has never been published. Before his death, however, it was Nathan Darby's wish that you see what we saw.

Step 1: Observing the condition of the prints.

The first print shown on page 213 is the "rolled print" of Malcolm Wallace, taken during his booking for the 1951 murder case. It is definitely the clearest of the two prints we will be examining. The second print, shown next on page 214 is the box #29 print.

10. Little Finger

Work Copy

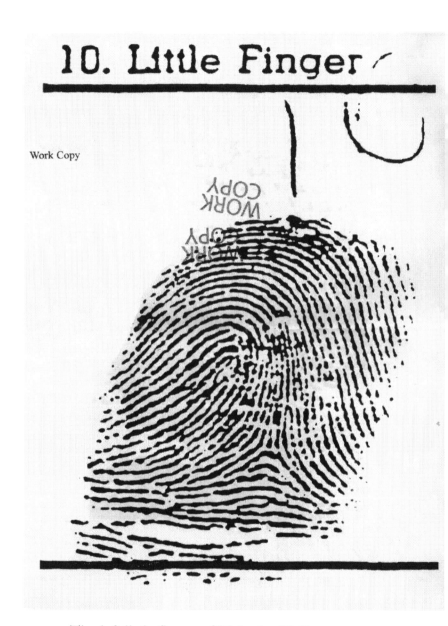

The left little finger of Malcolm Wallace

Work Copy

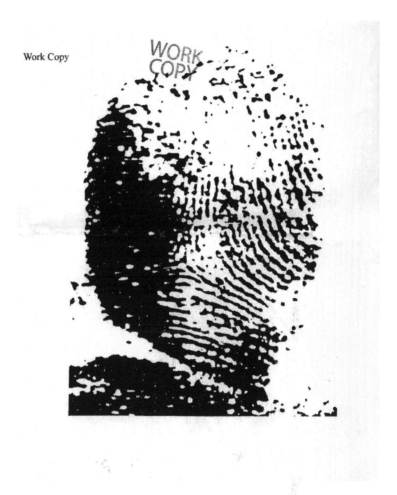

The "Box 29" print taken from the sixth floor.

Now, look at your LEFT little finger. Amazingly all of the information that lays before you was transferred from that tiny area. The rolled print, was of course made under controlled nearly perfect conditions, in a police station, under the supervision of a trained fingerprint officer. The latent print on page 214 was found on a cardboard box at the southeast window of the TSBD. It was made visible by chemical process. Before that, it was just a smudge of oils from someone's left little finger. Its clarity appears to be very poor. Much of it is indistinguishable. But amazingly – a portion of the print holds together, with some amount of clarity; enough perhaps for a trained examiner to draw a conclusion about the print. Because of the condition of the print, I firmly believe that there will never be a consensus of opinion on this fingerprint evidence.

Step 2: Examining the most striking similarity.

The first feature of these prints that I am about to point out is in my personal opinion, the most interesting. This area of the print seems to jump out as unusual. An area that is blank, with no ridges or detail visible. Darby suggests that this could be an injury area. Whatever the cause of this void, it is visible on both the rolled print and print #29 latent. Find point #7 on the rolled (left) print:

Blow up of Rolled print

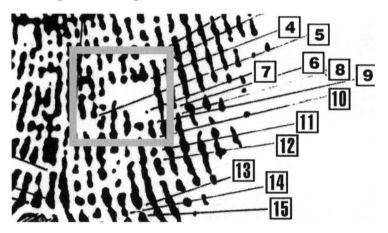

Point #7 sits near the bottom right corner of the grey outlined box above. Note that at the top of the box we see three or four descending ridges that stop abruptly – point #4 being one of them. Notice now that at the bottom of the box, a similar pattern occurs. Several ascending ridges stop abruptly – point #9 being one of them.

Points 9 and 10 form a stubby line with point # 7 being a small dot above it – much like the dot over an i.

Now, lets compare the latent (box 29) print:

Blow up of latent (box 29) print

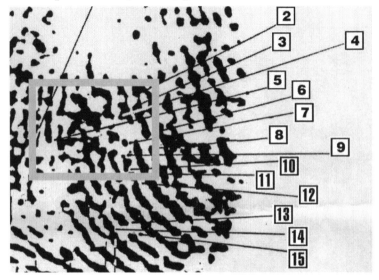

Again point #7 sits near the bottom right corner of the grey outlined box of the latent print. Note that similarly, at the top of the box we again see three or four descending ridges that stop abruptly – point #4 being one of them. (The similarities are obvious, even though this area is located in a very degraded portion of the print) Notice now that at the bottom of the box, a similar pattern occurs in the latent print. Several ascending ridges stop abruptly – point #9 being one of them - and, like the rolled print, points 9 and 10 form a stubby line with point # 7 being a small dot above it – like the dot over an i.

Step 3: Examining a second striking similarity.

Another area of similarity, like the first involves a void area where ascending and descending ridges terminate abruptly. Notice that this second area is to the left and slightly down from the first void area. Point #5 clearly terminates downward into this area. Point #1 (which looks like an upside down "V") points upward into this area.

Blow up of Rolled print

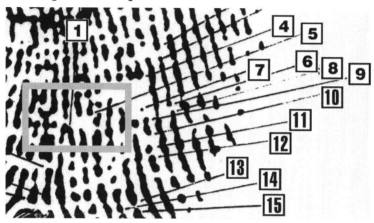

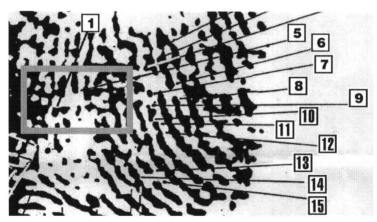

Blow up of latent print # 29. Do points 1 & 5 match?

Do you see the void area in both prints?

Step 4: Examining the 2 - 3 – 4 – 6 – 7 - 8 combo.

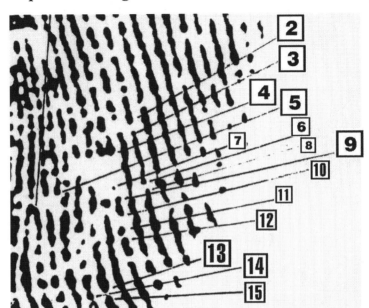

First, find the little point #7 in the above blowup of the rolled print. Now count two ridges to the right and stop. You should be at point #6. If you were to jump the gap downwards, you would land on point #8. But instead of going down, follow the ridge from point #6 upwards to the end of the ridge. You are now at point #3. Next, jump to the next point upwards, landing on point #2.

Latent print

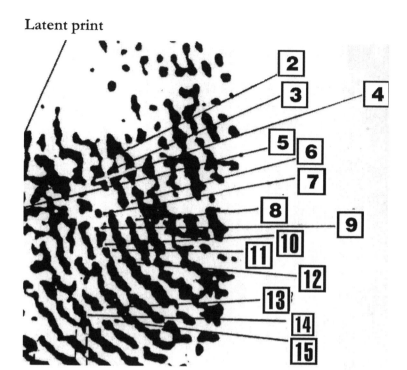

So now, let's try the same path on the latent print above. First, find the little point #7 in the above blowup of the rolled print. Count two ridges to the right and stop. You are now at point #6, right? If you were to jump the gap downwards, you would land on point #8. But instead of going down, follow the ridge from point #6 upwards to the end of the ridge. You are now at point #3. Next, jump to the next point upwards, landing on point #2. Some may say that the gap between points 2 and 3 appears connected – however this anomaly is due to the poor condition of the latent print.

Step 5: Examining point #22 and its neighbors.

Blow up of Rolled print.

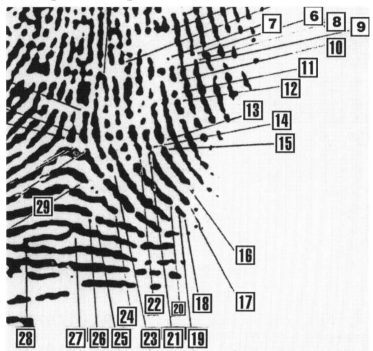

Point #22 is an "ending ridge" – it is shown above, descending between two other ridges, where it ends. To the right of #22 is point #21, which descends down to #17. To the right and upwards from #17 is a small dot #16. Follow the ridge upwards from #16 and you come to #15. Jumping the gap up from #15 brings you to #13. Move one ridge to the left of #13 will bring you to point #14.

Now let's compare the latent print #29.

Blow up of latent print #29

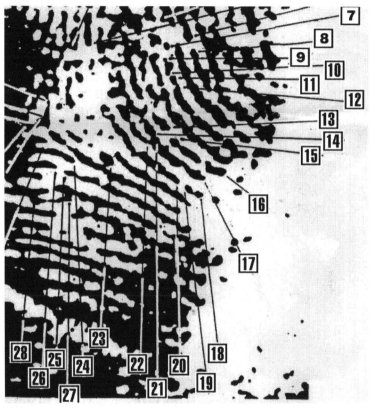

Point #22 on the poor quality latent above appears to touch the ridge to the right of it. But Darby notes that this is not the case. Most likely this is a ridge **ending**, NOT a bifurcation as it appears. To the right of #22 is point #21, which also appears blurred. It descends down to #17. To the right and upwards from #17 is a small dot #16. Follow the ridge upwards from #16 and you come to #15. Jumping the gap up from #15 brings you to #13. Move one ridge to the left of #13 will bring you to point #14.

The Men On The Sixth Floor

Let's look at some more of point #22's neighbors on the next page.

For this final section of our print review, I will use the last work that Darby did with the fingerprint. He mailed these to me a few weeks after our visit with him in Austin. Using a different set of numbers, Darby concentrates on points 61 thru 67, combined with old points 22 and 23. I have cleaned up the numbered squares, but left the note that he added on both the rolled print and the latent, namely: "Ok for #22 to touch ridge to right on latent print."

Blow up of Rolled print. (Darby's last analysis)

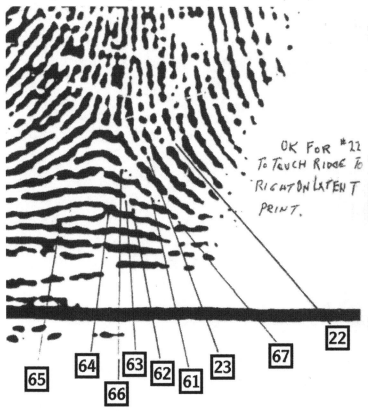

Start with point #66. Now drop down to the next ridge and follow it to the right until it ends at point #61. Next, drop down to the next ridge and go left until you come to the gap that separates points #62 and #63. Drop down one more ridge to point #64 which is a bifurcation or "fork in the road" that trails off to the left and ends at point #65.

At this point I will quote directly from Nathan's hand written notes to me: "Start at #64; right & down on ridge #64; #64 ends; count 4 ridges right; up 4th ridge; #22 is one ridge to the right."

Let's compare the latent print with the details cited above.

Blow up of latent print #29

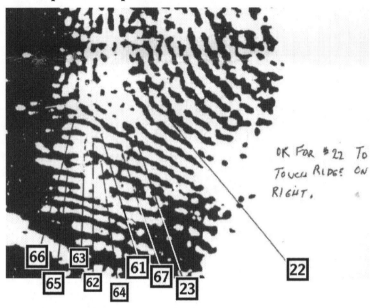

Start with point #66. See it barely sticking out from the indistinguishable mess on the left side of the print? Now drop down to the next ridge and follow it to the right until it ends at point #61. Next, drop down to the next ridge and go left until you come to the gap that separates points #62 and #63. Drop down one more ridge to point #64 which is a bifurcation or "fork in the road" that trails off to the left and ends at point #65. There is a lot of blotchiness in this area from point #63 area, on down, but you can still see bifurcation starting at point #64.

Again, quoting from Nathan's hand written notes: "Start at #64; right & down on ridge #64; #64 ends; count 4 ridges right; up 4th ridge; #22 is one ridge to the right." Can you see point #22 there to the right? Notice the hand written note to the right:

"OK for #22 to touch ridge on right"

Nathan's years of experience led him to determine that point #22 is NOT touching the ridge to its right. The poor quality of the latent print simply gives the untrained eye the impression that the two are touching when in actuality #22 is an "ending" ridge. Similar determinations are made quite often by experienced fingerprint experts. Take for example the case of the fingerprints of Lee Harvey Oswald.

During the Warren Commission hearings Sebastion Latona, an FBI fingerprint expert showed the commissioners two charts showing the comparison of Oswald's fingerprint and a latent print found on a paper bag found in the "snipers nest" area:

Mr. Eisenberg.

> Mr. Latona, in making these ridge counts, do you also pay attention to the so-called, let's say, geographical relation, the spacial relation of the two points?

Mr. Latona.

> Very definitely. Now, it does not always follow that the so-called geographical position will coincide exactly the same. That would be caused because of variations in the pressure used when the print was made. For example, when you make a print on a fingerprint card: when the inked print was made, the print was made for the specific purpose of recording all of the ridge details. When the print was left on the paper bag, it was an incidental impression. The person was not trying to leave a print In fact, he probably did not even know he left one. So the pressure which is left, or the position of the finger when it made the print, will be a little different. Accordingly the geographical area of the points themselves will not always coincide. But they will be in the general position the same.

Mr. Eisenberg.

> Mr. Latona, without going into detail, there are some apparent dissimilarities on the two sides of that chart. Can you explain why there should be apparent dissimilarities?

Mr. Latona.

> The dissimilarities as such are caused by the type of material on which the print was left, because of the pressure, because of the amount of material which is on the finger when it left the print. They would not always be exactly the same. Here again there appears a material difference in the sense there is a difference in coloration. This is because of the fact that the contrast in the latent print is not as sharp as it is in the inked impression, which is a definite black on white, whereas here we have more or less a brown on a lighter brown.

Mr. Eisenberg.

> Now, Mr. Latona, when you find an apparent dissimilarity between an inked and a latent print, how do you know that it is caused by absorption of the surface upon which the latent print is placed, or by failure of the finger to exude material, rather than by the fact that you have a different fingerprint?

Mr. Latona.

> That is simply by sheer experience.

Mr. Eisenberg.

> Would you say, therefore, that the identification of a fingerprint is a task which calls for an expert interpretation, as opposed to a simple point-by-point laying-out which a layman could do?

Mr. Latona.

> Very definitely so; yes.

The final analysis of the Malcolm Wallace fingerprint will be made by you, the reader. I have given you the print information that Darby entrusted to me. You have examined his expert interpretation.

I hope that the issue has been clarified for you.

In his last communication with me, Nathan wrote these words —

"There are 34 matching points; how can there be any question?"

I believe you Mr. Darby.

Chapter 21
Conclusions

"So...who do you think killed Kennedy?" We get asked that question all the time. When Mark and I first began this long project, we had no idea of who Kennedy's murderers might have been, aside from Loy Factor's story that the School Book Depository team consisted of four individuals, including himself and Oswald. We knew that at least two gunmen fired from separate windows on the sixth floor. We also assumed from Factor's statements, that the female conspirator, operating a walkie-talkie from her sixth floor position, was in contact with another shooter, or team of shooters - quite possibly in the stockade fence area of Dealey Plaza. Aside from these conclusions, we had no idea of who these individuals actually were, or who they took orders from. As to the motives of these killers, our guesses would have been no better than scores of other researchers, writers and investigators who have advanced countless ideas and theories. As mentioned earlier, we entered into this investigation with no preconceived ideas of who masterminded the assassination, or what the motives of the killers might have been.

By systematically following up on Loy Factor's story, we were able to determine not only the identity of the Depository shooters, but most important - who was behind the assassination! (Something that Loy was not aware of until our last interview on March 19, 1994, a few weeks before his death.) Subsequent discovery of various important pieces of information, gathered carefully over a three-year period of time gradually formed and strengthened our opinion.

The road led directly and without obstruction to Lyndon Johnson. Everywhere we looked, we found indicators of Johnson's involvement. But none of this information would have been attainable had it not been for the foundation testimony of Loy Factor.

From the very beginning of Loy's account, clues began pointing toward LBJ. For example, the very location where Loy first met Wallace - at the funeral of Sam Rayburn in Bonham, Texas. There was no other man that was more important to Lyndon Johnson than Rayburn. History shows that Sam Rayburn was Johnson's mentor, as well as a lifelong friend. For Wallace to be in attendance at Rayburn's funeral would be a natural occurrence for someone who was so close and loyal to LBJ.

To describe Malcolm Wallace as a Johnson loyalist would be a vast understatement, for in five weeks from the date of Rayburn's funeral, Wallace would murder Henry Marshall, the uncontrollable bureaucrat, who jeopardized Vice-President Johnson's political career.

Perhaps the most important revelation from Factor was the name "Wallace". The same evening following our second interview with Loy, the very mention of the name "Wallace" to Larry Howard (at the JFK Assassination Information Center) set off a chain of events that led to our introduction to Madeleine Brown, and subsequently the positive identification of Malcolm Everett Wallace. Once Wallace was identified as the recruiter of Loy Factor and the second gunman on the sixth floor, Johnson's influence became more obvious.

Coupled with Madeleine's claim that Lyndon Johnson alluded to the murder of President Kennedy the evening before the assassination, one cannot help but assign LBJ the role of conspirator number one.

The 1984 grand jury testimony of Billie Sol Estes, showing Lyndon Johnson's predisposition to contract for murders, and Malcolm Wallace's blind obedience in carrying out such murders, further strengthened our assertions of Johnson's involvement.

The 1952 trial of Malcolm Wallace for the murder of John Kinser illustrated the powerful protective influence Johnson exerted in behalf of his loyal followers. Using his massive political power, LBJ inserted his own top team of attorneys, installed a ringer in the jury and threatened the jurors. His political clout in Texas also assured that no reference to Johnson or his family would be mentioned in any newspaper article or news broadcast covering the Kinser murder trial.

And apparently the Johnson influence went even deeper. In Wallace's Naval intelligence file, supplied to us, (dated 20 July, 1961) Johnson is alluded to as bribing Bob Long, the prosecuting attorney in the case. The following quote is from page 4 of the 19 page file, paragraph 10. The SUBJECT referred to is Malcolm Wallace:

"Billy Roy WILDER and Richard C. AVENT, both assistant district attorneys who assisted in the procurement of SUBJECT's file, added their comments concerning rumors which persisted at the time of SUBJECT's trial. WILDER alleged that Bob LONG, former district Attorney, was reported to have been the recipient of valuable property in the city of Austin as a result of his suppression of certain aspects involving political ramifications. "

In 1996 we released portions of the "Estes documents", adding further support to the participation of Lyndon Johnson in the assassination. These documents, now complete, independently verify the story that was made public by Loy Factor - that Malcolm Wallace recruited the assassins of John F. Kennedy and not only organized the assassination but participated in it.

We have shown that Lyndon Johnson was a man not afraid to employ murder as a means of protecting or advancing his interests. But what were his motives in the murder of JFK?

In the assassination of President Kennedy, the same question must be asked as in any other crime, namely, who would benefit most from this murder? The answer to this question is Lyndon Johnson - for several reasons:

Stated quite simply, Johnson wanted to be the President of the United States more than anything else in the world. As many authorities on LBJ will attest, this dream was one that started at an early age and continued throughout his whole life. There was nothing that could stand in his way. He purportedly used every possible means, including campaign fraud, buying votes, and stuffing ballot boxes, to gain political victories. He occasionally even bragged about his stolen victories. His political backers, mainly rich Texas businessmen, were rewarded handsomely for helping him reach his goal with lucrative government contracts and sweetheart deals.

Johnson's loss to John Kennedy at the 1960 Democratic Convention came to him as a shocking surprise. His acceptance of the vice-presidential spot was in effect a last-ditch attempt to position himself for the presidency, knowing that he would be only a heartbeat away from the Oval Office.

Another important motive for Johnson to have John Kennedy assassinated would be to quench the investigations into his own scandalous activities that plagued him at the time. In 1963 Johnson became embroiled in so much scandal that even the Kennedys wanted to cut their losses and rid themselves of him. Johnson's problems had embarrassed the administration and the word was out that he would be dumped as vice president in 1964. Frantic, LBJ faced two options: either be sucked in to the bottomless pit of political scandal, thereby losing even his vice presidential status and resigning in shame, or - have Kennedy eliminated, ascend to the office of the president, and thereby quench all pending investigations. He had everything to gain from the latter choice and he made it with brazen LBJ confidence.

Johnson had been implicated in three major scandals - the Estes scandal, the TFX/General Dynamics affair, and in November of 1963, the Bobby Baker Scandal was at its peak. In fact, congress was in the middle of investigating the Johnson /Baker connection on the very day of the assassination. But an amazing thing happened after the assassination of President Kennedy. All of the investigations into the above-mentioned scandals lost their momentum and were quietly brought to a close! Johnson's strategy proved to be faultless - he became the most powerful leader on earth and avoided indictment simultaneously. Someone once said, "To commit the perfect crime, you don't have to be intelligent, just in charge of the investigation that follows."

Financial reward was another strong motivator for LBJ. At the time of Lyndon Johnson's death, his estate was reportedly worth between 10 and 20 million dollars. Johnson not only benefited personally from his powerful political position, but was able to reward handsomely many of his long-time supporters (such as the Brown and Root Company) by directing and influencing the award of multi-billion dollar government contracts along the way. A Texas attorney once noted, "To understand Lyndon Johnson, you have to get down to the Brown and Root of the matter." Yes, the rich Texas oilmen, contractors and businessmen were his kind of men, and he was their kind of president.

The men on the sixth floor have all been silenced. One, Lee Harvey Oswald, was immediately eliminated by Jack Ruby, on November 24, 1963. Malcolm Wallace, at age 50 perished in a single car accident in east Texas in 1971. Loy Factor, silenced by fear for nearly three decades, lived longer that any of the known conspirators, until he too was silenced by illness. Perhaps that is precisely the reason that he revealed what he knew - he lived the longest. Would Oswald or Wallace eventually have talked, had they too lived? I think they might have.

And what of the woman on the sixth floor? Young Ruth Ann, the cold-hearted coordinator of the plot, remains as much a mystery today as she did to Loy Factor on the day in November 1963, when he first met her. Because of her youth at the time of the assassination, it is quite possible that she is still alive, and in her late fifties. But like Factor, whose life was a hard fought tumultuous event and Wallace who turned to the booze to numb his pain, Ruth Ann, if alive, is likewise enduring a rueful existence. Perhaps she too will someday come forward to elaborate on the Loy Factor story.

There are, we strongly feel, individuals still alive that hold in their memories the details that could completely "flesh out" the present day skeleton we have introduced to the public. Of these, perhaps the most important is Billie Sol Estes. He has testified under oath that it was Lyndon Johnson himself that ordered the murder of Henry Marshall at the hand of Malcolm Wallace. It is understandable that he has remained silent about these things for all these years, considering his time spent in court, as well as in prison. Nonetheless Estes remains a treasure-trove of information about LBJ's dark side. Having funneled millions of dollars to Johnson and others in exchange for preferential treatment, Estes (with immunity, if necessary) could "put history straight", by revealing all he knows about Malcolm Wallace, Lyndon Johnson and anyone else who may have been connected to the assassination of President Kennedy and its subsequent cover-up. By making public the secret tapes of LBJ's illegal activities, Estes could prove to the world that it was he that took the fall for Lyndon Johnson. My personal attempt to question Billie Sol about these matters has been to no avail. Others (including his own daughter) who have inquired about this particularly sensitive area in his life have met with similar results.

A further investigation into Malcolm E. Wallace needs to be continued by someone with more authority and resources than these two writers. More research needs to be directed towards determining who his circle of friends and primary associates were, because Wallace's acquaintances and friends tended to be LBJ's also. These connections bear further scruitiny.

Clifton C. Carter, implicated in the Marshall murder and the Kennedy assassination by Billie Sol Estes, is one deserving of a closer look. Carter, a former intelligence agent, commanded OSS operations in Italy during World War II.

After the assassination, Clifton C. Carter remained close to Johnson, staying overnight at his house for the next few days, and continued to meet with him each day in the White House during the first part of his presidency, although never actually working in the White House. There is much more to learn about his role in Johnson's criminal activities.

In January of 1994, while Mark and I were researching the Loy Factor account, Larry Howard passed away. Ours was one of the last projects that Larry worked on. Sadly, soon to follow was Loy Factor himself, on May 5th, 1994. Within the last few years we have lost Ike Altgens, Phil Willis, Charles Brehm, Harold Norman, John Connally, Senator Ralph Yarborough, Perry Russo and Richard Case Nagell - all important witnesses in this case. Time is running out! We have tried very hard to point the public towards an important new door of opportunity. Before all assassination witnesses disappear, there is an immediate need to open that door further. By narrowing down the search we also need to close a few old doors along the way. This book has been our attempt to do just that.

Glen Sample and Mark Collom

Made in the USA
Columbia, SC
28 December 2023

29592162R00130